Fred CELIMENE
Christophe PROVIDENCE

Dynamics of Digitalization and Inclusion

Fred CELIMENE
Christophe PROVIDENCE

Dynamics of Digitalization and Inclusion

Economic, Educational and Social Perspectives on Haiti

ScienciaScripts

Imprint
Any brand names and product names mentioned in this book are subject to trademark, brand or patent protection and are trademarks or registered trademarks of their respective holders. The use of brand names, product names, common names, trade names, product descriptions etc. even without a particular marking in this work is in no way to be construed to mean that such names may be regarded as unrestricted in respect of trademark and brand protection legislation and could thus be used by anyone.

Cover image: www.ingimage.com

This book is a translation from the original published under ISBN 978-620-6-72967-9.

Publisher:
Sciencia Scripts
is a trademark of
Dodo Books Indian Ocean Ltd. and OmniScriptum S.R.L publishing group

120 High Road, East Finchley, London, N2 9ED, United Kingdom
Str. Armeneasca 28/1, office 1, Chisinau MD-2012, Republic of Moldova, Europe
Managing Directors: Ieva Konstantinova, Victoria Ursu
info@omniscriptum.com

Printed at: see last page
ISBN: 978-620-3-28270-2

Contents

Presses de l'Institut Universitaire des Sciences (P-IUS)

Created as part of the modernisation of higher education and scientific research in Haiti, the Presses de l'Institut Universitaire des Sciences (P-IUS) aims to promote the production and dissemination of knowledge in spirit of academic excellence. Based on the strategic research areas defined by the Centre de Recherche Scientifique (CRS) for the period 2024-2029, the P-IUS is a space dedicated to the promotion of scientific and educational work.

The P-IUS editorial board, made up experts from a range of disciplines, guarantees the quality and relevance of publications. Its members include :

- Dr Jude-Mary St-Martin, Director of Presses de l'IUS and Head of Axis 1 of CRS-IUS research in Haiti;
- Dr Philippe Simon, Researcher at the CRS-IUS in Haiti and Deputy Director of the IUS Press;
- Dr Kiria DESPINOS, Researcher and Head of Axis 2 of the CRS-IUS Haiti research programme;
- Dr Nelson SYLVESTRE, University Professor and Head of Axis 3 Research at CRS-IUS Haiti;
- Dr Fred CELIMENE, University Professor and Head of Axis 4 Research at CRS-IUS Haiti;
- Dr Louis-Auguste JOINT, University Professor and Associate Researcher at CRS-IUS Haiti;
- Dr Cuauhtemoc OCHOA TINOCO, Associate Researcher at CRS-IUS Haiti;
- Dr Michel DISPAGNE, University Professor and Associate Researcher at the CRS-IUS in Haiti;
- Dr Christophe PROVIDENCE, Senior Lecturer and Researcher at CRS-IUS in Haiti;
- +33 PhD students in 2023-2024, Research assistants at the CRS-IUS in Haiti.

Through an interdisciplinary approach and a commitment to international academic standards, P-IUS is committed to contributing to the development of knowledge in Haiti and the region. For more information or to submit a proposal, please contact us:
Contact: contact@ius.education | Website: www.ius.education
Telephone: +509 44 64 28 28 / +596 696 91 24 81
Address: Delmas 29, Entrée Star 2000, 6110 Port-au-Prince, Haiti
A space dedicated to research, reflection and the dissemination of knowledge.

Statement of the problem

Digital technology has become a major vector of economic, social and cultural transformation on a global scale. In a global context of increasing digitalisation, Haiti finds itself at a crossroads where technological advances offer immense opportunities, but also pose considerable challenges. Information and communication technologies (ICTs) are gradually penetrating the country's various sectors, transforming the way citizens interact with banking, education, health and other essential infrastructure services. However, this transition is taking place within a framework marked by structural inequalities, a fragile infrastructure and a lack of institutional coordination, amplifying the risks of exclusion for already vulnerable populations.

Against this backdrop, this collective work aims to explore the dynamics of digitalisation in Haiti through an interdisciplinary analysis encompassing economics, education and health. It brings together contributions from local researchers and experts who examine the impact of digitisation and ICTs on strategic areas of national development. Their aim is twofold: to assess the potential of digital technology to improve social inclusion, and to suggest ways of overcoming existing obstacles.

Context and issues

Haiti faces multiple challenges, including a stagnant economy, deep social inequalities and limited access to modern infrastructure. These structural problems are holding back the country's ability to exploit the full potential of ICTs. For example, while digital banking could revolutionise the operations of small and medium-sized enterprises (SMEs), shortcomings in the quality banking services persist. Similarly, mobile money - a promising solution for induring unbanked populations - suffers from uneven adoption due to institutional tensions and a lack of digital education.

In the healthcare sector, medical information systems offer major prospects for improving data management and the effectiveness of care. However, their implementation remains fragmented, with major challenges linked to interoperability, technical resources and user training. At the same time, in higher education, the digital divide is accentuating inequalities, academic performance and the ability of institutions to meet the needs of students and teachers.

Objectives of the project

This book examines the dynamics of digitisation in Haiti through an approach structured into two main parts. The first part focuses on the economic and social aspects of digitalization, exploring the effects of digital banking, mobile money and health information systems. The second part examines the impact of ICT in higher education, focusing on the digital divide, teachers' perceptions and strategies for sustainable digital transformation in education.

Structure of the work

Each chapter is a unique contribution to the debate on digitalisation and inclusion in Haiti:

1. Quality of banking services and SME performance (analysis of the effect of digital banking on SMEs in Jacmel) ;

2. Mobile money and financial inclusion (study of institutional tensions and opportunities for reducing inequalities) ;

3. Health information systems at the crossroads: exploring the technical, social and organisational challenges facing healthcare systems);

4. Digital divide and academic performance (impact of digital inequalities on student success in higher education) ;

5. Teachers' perceptions and practices (the current state of ICT in university teaching and proposals for effective integration).

An interdisciplinary approach

The aim of this book is to offer a global and contextualised reflection on digitalisation in Haiti. By drawing on economic, social, educational and technological perspectives, it aims to propose concrete solutions to meet the challenges and maximise the opportunities presented by digital technology. It is aimed at researchers, policy-makers, teachers, students and professionals interested in the challenges of digital transition in a developing country.

By exploring the many facets of digitalisation, this book hopes to inspire strategic action for an inclusive and sustainable transformation in Haiti.

Part I

Digitalisation and Inclusion in the Social and Economic Sectors

Setting the context for Part One

Digitalisation and Inclusion in the Social and Economic Sectors

Digitalisation is a key driver of economic and social transformation in developing countries. In Haiti, where traditional infrastructures are struggling to meet people's needs, digital technologies are opening up new prospects for improving access to basic services, stimulating the economy and reducing inequalities. However, their implementation still faces structural, institutional and social challenges. This first part looks at the dynamics of digitalisation in strategic sectors such as finance and health, highlighting the opportunities and obstacles to their effective integration.

Context and relevance

In a country where a large proportion of the population is still excluded from traditional financial systems and has to contend with limited health services, digital technologies are emerging as powerful tools for bridging these gaps. Digital banking, for example, has the potential to transform the relationship between banks and small and medium-sized enterprises (SMEs), facilitating access to credit, improving financial management and boosting productivity. At the same time, the rise of mobile money offers an innovative solution for including unbanked populations, while meeting the need for fast, secure transactions.

In the healthcare sector, digital information systems enable better management of medical data and improved quality of care. However, their implementation in Haiti is hampered by problems of interoperability, inadequate infrastructure and training for healthcare professionals, all of which limit their impact.

Objectives of the game

This first part aims to analyse the impact of digitalisation on key economic and social sectors in Haiti, while assessing the conditions needed to maximise their benefits. The chapters in this part explore the following themes:

1. The effect of digital banking on the performance of SMEs, particularly in the context of the city of Jacmel, where SMEs are an important lever for local development.

2. A study of mobile money as a tool for financial inclusion, highlighting the challenges associated with institutional coordination and digital education.

3. The evaluation of health information systems at Carrefour, an illuminating case study of the constraints and opportunities of technology adoption in an environment of limited resources.

Approach and articulation

The chapters in this part take an interdisciplinary approach, combining economic, social and technical analyses. They use a variety of methods, ranging from field surveys to case studies, to provide a comprehensive and contextualised view of the issues surrounding digitisation in Haiti. By exploring these themes, this section aims to provide concrete ways of overcoming the obstacles and promoting the effective adoption of ICTs, while taking account of local realities.

The contributions in this section illustrate that, although digitisation presents significant opportunities for social and economic inclusion in Haiti, its success depends on concerted action between public, private and community players. The findings and recommendations presented in these chapters are intended to inspire appropriate strategies for sustainable development based on the potential of digital technologies.

Quality of Banking Services in Haiti: The Impact of Digitalisation on SME Performance in Jacmel

Mr Bertrand DESTINE
Research assistant, CRS-IUS Haiti.
Dr Philippe SIMON
Researcher at CRS-IUS in Haiti.

Introduction

The quality of banking services is generally defined as the gap between customers' expectations and their perceptions of the services offered by banks (Hafiane & Jed, 2021; Tsapi, 2020; Bahia & Nante, 2000). This concept refers to the notion of satisfaction, since it is understood from the point of view of customers making an overall judgement about the services after using them (Lakhrif et al., 2016; Boyer & Nefzi, 2009; Zeithaml, 1988). In general, the services offered by banks are many and varied; they include deposits, payments, credit, transfers, online services, etc.

In Haiti, there is considerable dissatisfaction with the quality of services offered by banks (World Bank, 2019). This is particularly felt by small and medium-sized enterprises (SMEs), which rely heavily on banking services to operate (Paul, Juma'h & Dorante, 2018). This dissatisfaction stems not only the high cost and scarcity of credit, but also from a series of malfunctions, linked above all to payment systems (recurring lack of liquidity, increased cheque clearing times, network breakdowns, etc.), making it more difficult for these businesses to operate. This, in turn, has an impact on their performance, which is seen here in its commercial dimension, and measured in terms of sales and the quality-cost-delivery time of goods or services.

In the literature, the link between the quality of banking services and the performance of SMEs has not been studied directly. The vast majority of work on this subject focuses mainly on bank financing. Opinions therefore divided. For some, bank financing increases the performance of SMEs (Kone & Thera, 2022; Etogo-Nyaga, 2020), while for others, bank credit decreases the performance of these businesses (Akitan, 2015; Tioumagneng, 2011). To our knowledge, no study has analysed the impact of bank malfunctions on the performance of SMEs. Similarly, research work has sought to understand the effect of banking digitalisation on the performance of SMEs, with the exception of the IDB (2011) for Costa Rica, which reveals that the use of internet banking does not increase the performance of micro and small enterprises (MPEs). However, digital banking is an essential technique that relies on the use of new digital technologies (social networks, mobile technologies and integrated data processing tools) to improve the customer experience and, consequently, the performance of customer businesses (Elouahabi & Dakkor, 2022; Driss, 2017).

We are therefore interested in understanding the phenomenon at a local level. We are seeking to determine the impact of digital banking on business performance, in a context marked by dysfunctions at the level of banks in Haiti. Our research question is as follows: what effect can digital banking have on the performance of SMEs in Jacmel? To answer this question, we formulate the following hypotheses:

- H1: Digital banking is a positive effect on the turnover of SMEs in Jacmel.
- H2: Digital banking is a positive effect on the quality-cost-delivery timescale of goods and services for SMEs in Jacmel.

The general aim of this study is to show the correlation between the quality of banking services and the performance of SMEs in Jacmel. More specifically, it aims to analyse the effect of digital banking on the performance of these businesses. Through this work, we hope to draw the attention of the leaders of the banking system to the need to provide quality services to SMEs, while exploiting new technologies, in order to contribute to their development and performance on the market. After all, business performance and development are largely influenced by the active participation of banks.

The methodological approach adopted is based on the principle that the services offered by banks to SMEs are not limited solely to credit (IFC-World Bank, 2010). It incorporates other variables likely to explain the performance of these businesses, such as payment services and digital services. With this in mind, we conducted a survey of a sample of 118 SMEs in Jacmel, not only to find out their perceptions of the services received from banks, but also to assess the impact of the quality of these services on their performance. Using appropriate econometric and statistical methods, we processed and analysed the data collected. The results obtained, with a few exceptions, confirm the hypotheses formulated.

This research paper is divided into six sections. The first seeks to highlight, through a brief literature review, the link between the quality of banking services, digitalisation and the performance of SMEs. The second deals with the quality of banking services in Haiti. The third examines the bank-SME relationship in Jacmel, while the fourth presents the data and methods used. Finally, the fifth and sixth sections analyse the effect of bank digitalisation on the performance of SMEs in Jacmel.

I. Link between the quality of banking services, digitalisation and the performance of SMEs

The economic and managerial literature is replete with articles dealing separately with the quality of banking services, the digitalisation of banking and the performance of SMEs. However, none of them has really attempted to establish a link between these different variables. In general, authors establish a link between bank financing, which is only one aspect of banking services, and SME performance, which leads to divergent conclusions. For some, the relationship between the two variables is positive. This is the case, for example, of Kone & Thera (2022) who, on the basis of a study carried out on 30 SMEs in the building and public works sector in Bamako (Mali), show that bank financing has a positive influence on the financial performance of these businesses, subject to a lower interest rate. They conclude that the more companies take on debt, the more efficient and profitable they are.

Long before them, Etogo-Nyaga (2020) obtained an almost similar result in Cameroon. Using statistical analysis and the multiple regression , the results of his work show that access to bank finance for an SME increases its probability of improving its performance. In fact, this probability rises from around 5.6/10 when the SME has no access to finance to almost 7/10 when it y has access. However, his econometric analysis puts the impact of access to finance on SME performance into perspective. Access to finance does have a positive but insignificant effect on the performance indicator. The quality and nature of the loans granted, which are always short-term and limited in amount, help to explain this result.

For other authors, on the contrary, the relationship between the two variables is negative. Akitan (2015), for example, is part of this trend. Carrying out a comparative analysis between Cameroon and Senegal, his study highlights the impact of bank credit on turnover, an indicator of business performance. Once the performance equation has been estimated, the results reveal a negative relationship between bank finance and business performance in these countries.

The conclusion of this study is not new. It follows on from that of Tioumagneng (2011), which sought to analyse the relationship between the maturity of bank loans and business performance, using Cameroon as a case study. The results show that long-term bank debt, against all expectations, is detrimental to business performance. The transactional behaviour of banks in the experimental area under consideration is the cause.

That said, apart from bank finance, there are no other studies that have sought to incorporate or use other aspects of banking services to explain SME performance. The only study that attempts to link the quality of banking services and SME performance, outside of bank finance, is that of the IDB (2011), which establishes a link between the use of internet banking and SME performance in Costa Rica. Using an experimental method with systematically randomised participants, this study seeks to determine whether the use of online services by SME customers of the National Development Bank has an impact on their performance. As performance is a complex, polysemic and multidimensional concept (Issor, 2017; Sangue-Foto & Wamba, 2017), it is measured here in terms of productivity, increased sales and reduced business costs. The results show that use of and access to the internet is limited in SMEs, and in no case does this lead to an increase in sales, productivity or a reduction in costs. It should be stressed, however , that the study only takes into account one aspect of digitalisation. It not include other elements, such as the use of bank cards, for example, which we are considering in the case of Haiti.

II. Quality of banking services in Haiti

In Haiti, the quality of services offered by banks is synonymous with dissatisfaction for many SME customers. This means that their expectations are not being met terms of the perceptions they have of these services. These perceptions are negative in many respects, as revealed by the reactions of these businesses (Paul, Juma'h & Dorante, 2018). One of the reasons for this dissatisfaction is the quality of the credit. The credit offered by banks to SMEs is expensive, scarce and concentrated. Several studies demonstrate this. Doura (2012), for example, provides detailed information on the characteristics of credit. But one of the studies that highlights the issue of the concentration of bank credit in Haiti is that of Ambroise (2019). By analysing credit cycles and economic activity from 1980 to 2016, she shows that banking institutions largely finance less risky sectors, such as trade, to the detriment of other sectors with higher added value, such as agriculture. This, combined with political unrest and natural disasters, among other factors, has had a negative impact on economic activity. The concentration of credit is not only sectoral, but also geographical, with provincial towns more disadvantaged than the capital (Cadet, Providence, & Antenord, 2018).

Moreover, it is not just the quality of credit that is at the root of SME dissatisfaction. The malfunctions that banks have been experiencing for some time are a major factor. These problems affect the banks' payment systems, which are essential for businesses. Indeed, no business, in its relations with the bank, can function without payments from the bank. However, the dysfunctions observed are characterised above all by a lack of liquidity, an increase in the time taken to clear cheques and a lengthening of the time taken to make transfers available, particularly on bank premises.

First of all, it should be pointed out that the lack of liquidity is reflected in the inconvertibility of deposits and currency. For some time now, banks have been imposing limits on withdrawals of cash - whether in gourdes or US dollars. These limits are neither communicated nor formally explained, and vary both from day to day and from customer to customer. It is true that companies have other means of carrying out transactions, such as bank transfers or cheques. However, because of their generally management methods and their relationship with certain preñantes, such as wholesalers, they are sometimes forced to use cash, which seems more convenient for certain transactions. As a result, when they cannot obtain cash immediately, they turn to other solutions that can be costly in terms of time and money, which ultimately affects the quality of their products. This is why, in order to adapt to the situation and get around the banking anomalies, some companies are inventing other ways of operating (such as, for example, conserving as much cash as possible), which can prove risky.

The national currency is in a difficult position on the foreign exchange market. The trend is for it to depreciate against the US dollar, which is also circulating in the economy. This phenomenon of dual currency circulation, which is a headache for the monetary authorities, is affecting the quality of services offered by banks. SMEs are finding it difficult to exchange money on the banking market. Not only are there limits on buying and selling dollars, but the rates charged by banks are unfavourable to them. As a result, to get round the difficulties of the banking market, some SMEs are turning to the informal market to meet their needs, thereby fuelling pressure and speculation on the dollar, and hence its scarcity. This inevitably complicates their operations, with all the consequences that entails.

Then there is the increase in the time taken to clear cheques and the time taken to make transfers available, which in practice means that the amounts corresponding to payment orders take longer than usual to be available in the accounts. These problems are due to both technical factors (linked to the banking system itself) and economic factors (linked to the climate insecurity in the country). Official notes published on this subject leave no doubt. As a result, companies are experiencing major delays in out their operations. They may take several days to receive payments from their customers or make payments to their suppliers.

Some suppliers may even refuse to accept cheques made payable to them in payment of orders or invoices, as they will have difficulty in obtaining the funds within the desired timeframe. This creates problems for businesses. That's why a number of them have got into the habit of using online services. It seems that these services are less affected by the banks' payment problems. But despite this, many are not using them in Jacmel.

III. Jacmel, banking and SMEs

Jacmel is a city of almost 40,000 inhabitants, located in the South-East department of Haiti. It is known worldwide as a cultural and tourist city. In 2014, it was designated a Creative City by UNESCO, a testament to its excellence in the creative fields. However, Jacmel is also a commercial city. It owes this character to its history, as, in the past, it was the hub of the country. According to the latest census conducted by the Ministry of Commerce and Industry in 2014, there were 1,082 businesses in the city, far more than in most other provincial towns.

This figure tends to change, but because of the persistent crisis over the years (with the creation of some businesses and the closure of others), the difference should not be substantial ten years on. It should be pointed out that all of these businesses are micro and small enterprises, if categorised at all. However, for the purposes of this study, we consider that MSEs are an integral part of SMEs (ILO, 2015; IFC-World Bank, 2010; OECD, 2004).

The history of banking in Jacmel is a recent one. Until the late 1980s, there was only one branch of the Banque Nationale de Crédit (BNC) in the town. Its role was limited in relation to the legal remit of this state-owned bank, and consisted solely of receiving customer deposits, making payments and, to a certain extent, granting loans. In fact, it was not until the early 1990s that private commercial banks began to penetrate the city.

Of the eight banks operating on the market in 2024, four have a branch in Jacmel, and these happen to be the top four in the banking system: Unibank, Sogebank, BNC and Capital Bank. In terms of spatial distribution, the branches are all located at the bottom of the town centre. They serve an entire department with 10 communes and 2,658 businesses (MCI, 2014). Even so, very few of these businesses have access to their various services.

Banks offer a wide range of services to SMEs in Jacmel. They are almost identical to those offered in Latin America and mentioned in the IFC-World Bank surveys (2010). They include different types of account, credit cards, online services, loans, insurance and more. To y access them, SMEs must comply with the requirements and procedures established by the banks.

In general, these procedures vary little from one bank to another, as banks are required to comply with compliance standards set by the regulatory authorities (in particular the central bank) or by the networks and associations to which they belong. However, in some cases, particularly where businesses - for reasons of formality or other factors - do not have a bank account, the owner-managers use their own accounts to benefit from banking services. This is because SMEs, especially microenterprises, are often personalised and closely identified with their owner-managers (Barbot-Grizzo, 2012). However, the owner-managers are well aware that their businesses will not be able to benefit from certain services in this way.

That said, the perception of Jacmel's SME customers with regard to the quality of banking services seems rather negative. These businesses have to contend not only with the limited availability of credit, but also with malfunctioning payment systems. It should also be pointed out that there are other problems that accompany these anomalies, such as the banks' lack of communication, their lack of transparency, and the way customers are received and treated. All these factors influence the perception of customers, who disapprove of the quality services offered by banks. This is undoubtedly one of the reasons a significant number of SMEs are also turning to savings and credit cooperatives (CECs), which are positioning themselves as providers of alternative financial services, although they also have their own limitations. The data shows that this sector is booming in the Sud-Est department. Jacmel, for its part, has two CECs among the twenty largest in the country, out of the seventy-eight that make up the Haitian mutual microfinance landscape (BRH, 2018). As a result, businesses are trying to get by by any means necessary, because, beyond the problem of credit, bank malfunctions are not without consequences for their performance.

IV. Data and methods

The data collected for this study comes a questionnaire administered to 118 SMEs in the city. This questionnaire is structured in three parts and includes forty-five questions relating to the general information of the businesses surveyed, the services they receive from banks, and the impact of the quality of these services on their performance. The variables to be measured are therefore the performance of the SMEs, which constitutes the explained variable, and the banking services, which constitute the explanatory variables.

Performance refers to turnover and the quality-cost-delivery time (QCD) of goods or services provided by SMEs. Banking services include financing, payment services and digital services offered by banks. These services are measured using the indicators presented in the table below. It should also be noted that the survey focuses on the period from 2018 to 2023.

Tableau 1.   Banking services and indicators

Banking services	Indicators
Financing	Lending rate
	Loan amount
	Loan term
Payment services	Cheque cashing Interbank

	transfer
Digital services	Online service
	Credit card

Sources: Authors' calculations based on 2023 data

1. Sampling

There are no up-to-date data on the number of SMEs in Jacmel. Those that are available come from the MCI census carried out in 2014. According to this census, the number of SMEs operating in Jacmel is 1,082. It was on this basis that the sample of 118 SMEs was selected, representing 10.91% of the total. It should be emphasised that these are only formal SMEs.

The sample was drawn using two commonly used methods: the simple random method and the reasoned choice method. The simple random method, by definition, is a technique in which each element of the population has an equal chance of being selected. It is a probabilistic sampling method based on the principle of randomisation or random selection. The purposive method, on the other hand, involves collecting data without relying on a pre-established list of individuals in the population to be studied. This is a non-probabilistic method that relies on the knowledge and judgement of the interviewer. In the first case, a list of SMEs well known in the city for their size, activities and social weight was drawn up. The companies surveyed were selected from this list. In the second case, the SMEs were selected in the field on the sole criterion that they were legally recognised. However, it should be pointed out that certain techniques were implemented in order to maximise the probability of selecting formal SMEs, i.e. those likely to have relations with banks. These techniques are based on observation and appearance.

Other selection techniques were used. These consisted of selecting SMEs in all the major sectors of activity and in all areas of the city. Naturally, small businesses located in communal sections were deliberately neglected, as in the vast majority of cases these are small informal farming units. In Haiti, any unit that is not registered with the DGI, i.e. does not have a licence, is considered to be informal. The patente has a dual function: the one hand, it establishes the legal recognition of activities; and on the other, it serves as a tax and collection instrument, since it defines the economic unit as a taxpayer (Lamauthe-Brisson, 2002).

However, the patent is not enough to open bank accounts; recognition by the Ministry of Trade and Industry is also required. In other words, the small agricultural units in the communal sections cannot have relations with the banks and are therefore not eligible for selection. The SMEs that have been selected, on the other hand, are of mixed size. The main sectors in which they operate are: Construction, Hardware, Furniture, Hospitality, Bars and Restaurants, Pharmaceuticals, Cosmetics, Car and Motorcycle Spare Parts, Food and Beverages, Shopping Centres, Markets, etc.

2. The data collection process

To collect the data, a two-stage approach was adopted. Firstly, a surveyor was recruited to take part in the operations. His role was to help set up the data collection process and collect the data. To do this, he first had to organise the questionnaires and then prepare for his field trip. The interviewer, who had already taken part in previous surveys and had a certain strength of persuasion, received training in the administration of the survey and the content of the questionnaire. His recruitment was necessary, as it was decided to distribute the questionnaires to the physical addresses of the SMEs.

Logistical support was therefore needed. The option of sending the questionnaires by email via Google Forms or some other method was ruled out, for the simple reason that many SMEs in Jacmel do not have an email address. Many of those that do, do not seem to use it regularly. It was therefore safer to reach the SMEs in person, in order to get as many responses as possible. The advantage of this process was the direct interaction with the owner-managers, some of whom volunteered to provide additional details relating to the subject of the survey.

A total of 250 questionnaires were distributed. Of these, 124 were recovered, including 6 that were invalid due to missing or contradictory information. To carry out the distribution of questionnaires, a breakdown was made by SME location zone. Eleven major zones were identified. They are as follows: 1. Bassin Caiman-Pasquette-Dumeuze; 2. Beaudouin-Aviation- Orangers; 3. Bréman-Meyer-Cyvadier; 4. Centre-ville; 5. Labidou-Lamandou- Cap des Maréchaux; 6. Monchill-Sainte-Hélène; 7. Portai! Bainet; 8. Portai! la Gosseline; 9. Portai! Léogane; 10. Portai! St-Cyr; and 11. Siloé-Mome Ogé.

From Monday to Saturday, during regular business hours, the enumerator walked these areas to distribute and collect the forms. However, this exercise was not without its difficulties. A number of obstacles were encountered with certain SME owner-managers who, for various reasons, refused to cooperate. However, persuasive strategies were put in place to get a significant number of participants on board. The data collection period ran from 24 May to 20 June 2024. The valid response rate was 47.20%.

3. *The data collected*

The data collected is both quantitative and qualitative. Quantitative data includes, for example, turnover, interest rates, loan amounts and loan duration. Qualitative data refers to SMEs' perceptions of the quality banking services, their level of satisfaction with these services, and an estimate of the impact of banking malfunctions on the quality-cost-delivery time triptych for SMEs' products. These data will be used to measure the variables to be linked.

In addition, two main types of data are used in this study: secondary data and primary data. The secondary data refers all existing documents on the subject, such as the MCI census (2014) and the various BRH reports. Primary data comes from data collected in the field. Once collected, these data are consolidated in a database. This database is first created in Excel and then exported SPSS for processing and analysis.

4. *The models*

Two multiple regression models were used to carry out the econometric estimations. In the first, the variable explained, namely performance, is measured in terms of SME sales. In the second, it is measured in terms of the quality-cost-delivery time triptych of these companies' products. The models are specified as follows

Model 1	Model 2
PER = f (QSB)	PER = f (QSB)
Where PER: Performance of SMEs and QSB: Quality of banking services QSB = TI + MP+ DP + SBP + SD	Where PER: Performance of SMEs and QSB: Quality of banking services QSB = TI + SBP + SD
Therefore :	Therefore :
PERi = βα+ ß1TIi+ ß2MPi+ ß3 DP¡ + ß4SBPi + ß5SDi + sì	PERi = βα+ ßiTIi+ ß2SBPi+ ß3SDi + s¡
With	**With**
TI: Lending rate	TI: Lending rate
MP: Loan amount	SBP: Payment banking services
DP: Loan period	SD: Digital services
SBP: Payment banking services	βα: Constant
SD: Digital services	ß: Parameter vectors
βα: Constant	sí: Residual error i: Company index
ß: Parameter vectors	
sì : Residual error i : Company index	

It is important to note that, in the second model, performance is a dichotomous variable. It takes the value 0 if banking services lead to a drop in quality, a drop in sales and an increase in delivery time for SMEs, and the value 1 in the opposite case. Unlike the first model, only the variables interest rates, payment services and digital services are taken into account. The amount of the loan and the duration of the loan, which are in fact control variables, do not add any value in the estimation of the second model.

In addition, because of the theoretical and empirical links between the explanatory variables and the variable being explained, positive or negative signs are expected. All of this is presented in the table below.

Tableau 2.   Link between variables and company performance

Variable	Theoretical and empirical link with company performance	Expected sign
Interest rate	According to studies other than that of (Kone & Thera, 2022), the interest rate generally has a negative impact on company performance.	
Montani loan	Just by increasing capital, loan montani has a positive impact on business performance (Etogo-Nyaga, 2020).	+
Loan term	The duration of the loan tends to have a positive relationship with company performance; in fact, the longer it is, the better the performance, contrary to Tioumagneng (2011), the shorter it is, the poorer the performance. The second proposition is retained in this study.	
Payment services	In this study, payment services are characterised by a lack of liquidity and various problems that prevent cheques from	

	being cashed and transfer orders from being executed on time. A negative relationship is therefore expected with performance.	
Digital services	Unlike payment services, digital services appear to be better for business users. A positive relationship is expected with performance.	+

Sources: Authors' calculations based on 2023 data

V. Analysis of the effect of digital banking on the performance of SMEs in Jacmel

Digitalisation of banking has certainly had an impact on the performance of SMEs in Jacmel. This effect will be analysed at three levels: descriptive, explanatory and interpretative. It will focus on the determinants of business performance, statistical correlation, and the results of econometric models, followed by their interpretation. But first, let us present the general characteristics of the sample.

1. *General characteristics of the sample*

The SMEs selected to make up the study sample have some general characteristics that should be presented. These characteristics will make it easier to understand them and to place them in the overall context of the study. They concern both the specific characteristics of the SMEs (type, sector activity, number of years in existence, size, turnover) and the socio-demographic characteristics of the owner-managers (gender, age, level of education).

The sample data shows that 92.37% of SMEs are sole proprietorships, 3.39% are partnerships and 4.24% are limited companies. This confirms, as have many previous studies, that the national economic fabric is dominated by SMEs owned by individuals or families.

The data also show that a large proportion of these businesses in Jacmel operate in the Food-Beverages (30.51%) and Construction-Hardware-Furniture (27.12%) sectors. The other 9 sectors of activity include: Hotels-Bars-Restaurants (9.32%), Car and Motorcycle Spare Parts (9.32%), Pharmaceuticals-Cosmetics (5.08%), Shopping-Centre-Market (5.08%), Fuel-Energy (2.54%), Communication-Telephony (2.54%), Cookery-Pastry (1.69%), Sport-Leisure-Events (0.85%), Art-Crafts (0.85%) and Other (5.08%). Together, these sectors represent only 42.37%.

In terms of number of years existence, 38.98% of SMEs are between 7 and 12 years old, 27.12% between 1 and 6 years old, 20.34% between 13 and 18 years old, 5.93% between 25 and 30 years old, 5.08% between 19 and 24 years old, and 0.85% between 31 and 36 years old. This data suggests that businesses are surviving relatively long and not closing after three years, as is often the case for many start-ups in the country. However, as time goes on, the number of start-ups decreases. Most are located in the city centre (33.90%) and Beaudouin-Aviation-Orangers (20.34%). This is because the city centre has always been a business centre, while Beaudouin became a strategic location after the main market was relocated in 2010, resulting a large number of businesses moving in.

In terms of size, 84.75% of SMEs have between 1 and 10 employees, while 15.25% have between 10 and 50 employees. This shows that all the companies in the sample can be classified as micro and small enterprises (MSEs). Of these employees, 60.71% are men and 39.29% are women. The small size of the companies is consistent with their turnover, if we refer to the classifications of the ILO (2015) or the OECD (2004). Indeed, 42.37% of them have an annual turnover of less than 14.4 million gourdes (100,000 euros), and 57.63% have an annual turnover of less than 1.4 billion gourdes (10 million euros).

However, according to World Bank criteria, the breakdown is as follows: 42.37% of businesses have annual sales of less than 13.2 million gourdes (US$100,000 for micro-businesses), 46.61% have annual sales of less than 396 million gourdes (US$3 million for small businesses), while 11.02% have annual sales of less than 1.9 billion gourdes (US$15 million for medium-sized businesses).

Furthermore, the owner-managers are not balanced in terms of gender. The data from the sample shows that the entrepreneurial sector in Jacmel is dominated by men, with 72.03% of entrepreneurs compared with 27.97% of women. This is corroborated by the results of a number of studies carried out at national level, although in some specific areas there are more women than men.

The data also shows that the vast majority of owner-managers are young, with 72.19% aged under 50. Those over 50 represent only 28.81%.

In terms of education, owner-managers are relatively advanced. We can see that 28.81% have reached second level, 30.51% professional level and 40.68% university level. had less than these levels. This may be related to the relative longevity of the companies, as owner-managers seem well equipped to manage difficulties, both internal and external (El Manzani et al., 2018).

2. *The determining factors*

The variables related to banking services, which are essential for explaining the performance of SMEs, are considered to be determining factors. These variables relate to financing, payment services and digital services.

First and foremost, it should be noted that the banking services used by SMEs are as follows: savings account (70.34%), current account (51.69%), online services (38.98%), credit cards (32.20%), transfers (30.51%), loans (16.10%), and perfect parity for term accounts, insurance and other services (0.85%).

The banks providing these services to SMEs are distributed as follows: Sogebank (67.80%), Unibank (63.56%), Capital Bank (38.14%) and BNC (27.12%). It should also be noted that 72.88% of SMEs surveyed have an account with at least two banks, while 2.54% have an account with each of the four banks operating in the city.

In terms of financing, only 16.10% of SMEs benefit from bank loans, a very low percentage for entrepreneurship and, consequently, local development. Of these businesses receiving loans, 52.63% have loans of less than 1 million gourdes, 36.84% have loans of between 1 million and 10 million gourdes, and 10.53% have loans of between 10 million and 100 million gourdes. In addition, only 4 of them have loans in

US dollars. Of these 4 companies, 3 have loans of less than US$25,000, and 1 has a loan of more than US$500,000. The lending banks are distributed as follows: Capital Bank (47.83%), Sogebank (30.43%), Unibank (17.39%) and BNC (4.35%). The loans are of several types: equipment (39.13%), cash (30.43%), property (21.74%) and mortgage (8.70%). The term of the loans varies according to the type of loan and the lending bank: less than one year (15.79%), between 1 and 2 years (26.32%), between 2 and 3 years (42.11%), between 3 and 4 years (5.26%) and 5 years or more (10.53%). The majority of loans (68.43%) are for between 1 and 3 years. Interest rates vary across the banking market. According to the data in the sample, it is between 7% and 30% for gourde loans, and between 9% and 12% for dollar loans. These data reflect those published in the various BRH reports for this indicator.

When it comes to payment services, the situation is fairly critical. According to the data in the sample, SMEs face the problem of bank liquidity with the following frequencies: always (15.25%), often (61.02%), rarely

(22.88%) and never (0.85%). These frequencies show the scale of the problem, since 76.27% of SMEs do not receive immediate liquidity when they request it. However, there is a caveat to be mentioned regarding cheque and transfer payments. For SMEs, the problem of the non-availability within the usual timeframe of the amounts of cheques deposited in the accounts is broken down as follows: always (2.54%), often (25.42%), rarely (27.12%), never (5.08%) and non-response (39.83%). As for the problem of transfers not being available within the regular timeframe, which is not too dissimilar to that of cheques, the breakdown was as follows: always (2.54%), often (22.03%), rarely (34.75%), never (4.24%) and no reply (36.44%).

It should be pointed out that the regular time taken to clear cheques is 2 days, while the time taken to execute local and international transfer orders is 2 and 3 days respectively. However, the actual time it takes for a cheque to clear, according to SMEs, is as follows: 3-4 days (29.66%), 4-5 days (11.86%), 5 days or more (14.41%) and no reply (44.47%). With regard to transfers, the actual times taken to carry them out are, at local level: 2-5 days (50.00%), 5 days or more (9.32%) and no response (40.68%); and at international level: 3-5 days (5.93%), 5-10 days (9.32%), 10 days or more (2.54%) and no response (82.20%). There is therefore a discrepancy between the responses concerning the non-availability of payments within the regular timescales and the non-availability of payments within the actual timescales. Payments seem to take longer than SMEs report. In addition, it appears that SMEs are less affected by problems relating to cheque deposits and account transfers. This can also be explained by the fact that many of them make less use of these services.

Digital services are far more attractive. If we look at credit cards, we see that they are better suited to the needs of SMEs. In fact, when asked whether it facilitates transactions, the SMEs surveyed replied as follows: always (37.78%), often (48.89%) and rarely (13.33%). What's more, they encounter almost no problems when using the card; 97.78% of these businesses confirm this. The same applies to online services. When asked whether they facilitate transactions, the responses were as follows: always

(37.50%), often (54.17%), rarely (6.25%) and never (2.08%). As with the credit card, 91.67% of SMEs rarely problems using these services. The problem is that the vast majority do not use them. As far as credit cards are concerned, only 38.14% have one, compared with 61.86% who do not. The main reasons given were they had never applied for one or thought they would be refused. As for online services, 40.68% use them, compared with 59.32% who do not. The reasons given by non-users were a lack of information or ignorance of how to use them.

3. *Statistical correlation*

On the basis of the above, it is possible to establish a relationship between the perceived quality of banking services and the performance of SMEs in Jacmel. This relationship is presented in the table below.

Thus, we can see that, overall, one level or another, 66.10% of businesses compared with 33.90% say that problems banking services delay the completion of their operations; 64.41% compared with 35.59% say that these problems reduce the quality of their services; 70.35% compared with 29.65% say that problems with banking services reduce their sales; and 62.72% compared with 37.28% say that these problems increase their costs. It is therefore easy to understand why the vast majority (91.53% in total) are not satisfied with the quality of service they receive from banks, although, curiously, a significant proportion of SMEs that have received bank loans seem to put this situation into perspective.

Tableau 3.   Relationship between perceived quality and the performance of SMEs in Jacmel

Question asked	Beaucou P	A pen	Very pen	Not all	No banking service problems	N= 118
Q42. Do problems with banking services delay the completion of your transactions?	32,20 %	33,90 %	20,34 %	5,08 %	8,48 %	100,00 %
Q43. Do problems with banking services reduce the quality of your services?	25,43 %	38,98 %	20,34 %	6,78 %	8,47 %	100,00 %
Q44. Do problems with banking services reduce your sales?	23,74 %	46,61 %	12,71 %	8,47 %	8,47 %	100,00 %
Q45. Do problems with banking services increase your costs?	22,89 %	39,83 %	18,64 %	10,17 %	8,47 %	100,00 %

Sources: Authors' calculations based on 2023 data

Tableau 4.   Level of satisfaction of SME customers in Jacmel

Question asked	Very satisfied	Satisfied	Pen satisfied	Not satisfied	N= 118
Q39. Are you satisfied with your bank's	0,00 %	8,47 %	55,93 %	35,60 %	100,00 %

services?

Sources: Authors' calculations based on 2023 data

Tableau 5.   Perception of SME customers in Jacmel regarding bank loans

Question asked	Many	A pen	Very lean	Not at all	N = 19
Q41. Does the loan improve your financial situation?	15,79 %	52,63 %	15,79 %	15,79 %	100,00 %

Sources: Authors' calculations based on 2023 data

VI. Results of the econometric models and interpretation

Model 1. The results are as follows:

Model Summary[1,]

Model	R	R Square	Adjusted R Square	Std. Error of the Estimate	Durbin-Watson
1	,373[a]	.1 39	.100	1 8639461 9.1 9	1.949

a. Predictors: (Constant). Loan term, Payment services, Interest rate, Digital services, Loan amount
b. Dependent Variable: Turnover

ANOVA[a]

Model		Sum of Squares	df	Mean Square	F	Sig.
1	Regression	6.277E+17	5	1.255E+17	3.613	005[b]
	Residential	3.891E-18	112	3 474E + 16		
	Total	4.519E+18	117			

a. Dependent Variable: Turnover
b. Predictors: (Constant), Loan duration, Payment services, Interest , Digital services, Loan amount

Coefficients

Model		Unstandardized Coefficients B	Std. Error	Standardized Coefficients Beta	t	Sig.	Collinearity Statistics Tolerance	VIF
1	(Constant)	71516502.954	25319079.680		2.825	.006		
	Interest rate	-2120366.086	4129338.900		-.075	-.513	.609	.367	2.722
	Payment services	80280354.809	46335515.928	.154	1.733	.086	.980	1.020
	Digital services	81829568.323	36010352.847	.209	2.272	.025	.916	1.091
	Loan amount	6.819	3.201	.249	2.130	.035	.564	1.772
	Term of loan	4726164.286	34859284.654	.023	.136	.892	.264	3.787

a. Dependent Variable: Turnover

From the results obtained, it is easy to see that the model is globally significant at the 5% threshold. Indeed, if we refer to the analysis of variance (ANOVA), we see that F = 3613 > F* (tabulated) = 2.29. The model estimate is therefore validated. The model estimate therefore validated. Secondly, the errors are not autocorrelated. The Durbin-Watson test proves this, with a coefficient of 1,949, which is very close to 2. Finally, multicollinearity between the explanatory variables is not detected.

Their VIF ranges from 1 to 4, with respective tolerance levels. Thus, the interest rate has a VIF of 2,722 with a tolerance of 0.367; payment services a VIF of 1,020 with a tolerance of 0.980; digital services a VIF of 1,091 with a tolerance of 0.916; the loan amount a VIF of 1,772 with a tolerance of 0.564; and the loan term a VIF of 3,787 with a tolerance of 0.264. The only drawback is the coefficient of determination R^2, which is rather low at 13.90%. However, this does not affect the overall significance of the model. It simply indicates that there are other variables likely to explain performance, but which were not taken into account in this study.

Secondly, once the model has been estimated, it is essential to examine the beta coefficients of the explanatory variables. These coefficients provide information about the relationship between the explanatory variables and the variable being explained. Their significance is determined by Student's t, a test commonly used for this purpose. The hypothesis (Ho) of a zero coefficient is tested against the alternative hypothesis (Hi) of a coefficient other than zero (positive or negative, the test being two-tailed). A coefficient is considered significant if the probability is less than the 5% threshold.

In this context, the results reveal that two variables have positive and statistically significant relationships with performance. These were loan amount (ß = 0.249, t = 2,130 and $p < 0.05$) and digital services (ß = 0.209, t = 2,272 and $p < 0.05$). This means that the loan amount and digital services have a positive influence on performance, with the expected signs.

Next, the results show that two other variables have positive relationships with performance, but these are not significant. These are loan duration (ß = 0.023, t = 0.136 and $p > 0.05$) and payment services (ß = 0.154, t = 1.733 and $p > 0.05$). These variables show signs contrary to expectations.

Finally, we find that the interest rate has a negative and statistically insignificant relationship with performance (ß = -0.075, t = -0.513 and $p > 0.05$). The expected sign of this relationship is therefore justified.

The performance equation can then be written as :

PERÌ = 71 516 502 954 - 0.075TIÌ + 0.249 MPi + 0.023 DPi + 0.154 SBPi + 0.029 SDi + s¡.

Model 2. The results are as follows:

Model Summary[0]

Model	R	R Square	Adjusted R Square	Std. Error of the Estimate	Durbin-Wats on
1	,307[a]	.094	.070	.452	1.626

a. Predictors: (Constant), Digital services. Payment services, Interest rates b. Dependent Variable: QCD

ANOVA[a]

Model		Sum of Squares	df	Mean Square	F	Sig.
1	Regression	2.427	3.809		3.953	.01 0[b]
	Residential	23.335	114	.205		
	Total	25.763	117			

a. Dependent Variable: QCD

b. Predictors: (Constant), Digital services, Payment services, Interest rates

Coefficients

Model		Unstandardized Coefficients B	Std. Error	Standardized Coefficients Beta	t	Sig	Collinearity Statistics Tolerance	VIF
1	(Constant)	1.110	.362		3.067	.003		
	Interest rates	-.024	.020	-.106	-1.183	.239	.994	1.006
	Payment services	-.332	.111	-.267	-2.993	.003	.999	1.001
	Digital services	.105	.084	.112	1.258	.211	.993	1.007

a. Dependent Variable: QCD

According to these results, the model is globally significant with a Fisher F = 3,953 and $p < 0.01$. The only concern remains the coefficient of determination $R^2 = 9.40\%$, which is very low, but somewhat understandable insofar as other variables likely to explain performance have not been taken into account. The residuals are not autocorrelated (DW = 1,626, close to 2) and the VIFs of the variables are between 1,001 and 1,007, exceeding the tolerance levels (0.993, 0.994 and 0.999). Furthermore, the beta coefficients show that payment services have a negative and highly significant relationship with performance (ß = -0.267, t = -2,993 and p < 0.01). This means that payment banking services have a negative impact on performance. It should also be noted that the relationship between the interest rate and performance is also negative, but this relationship is statistically insignificant (ß = -0.106, t = -1 183 and p > 0.05). The only variable in the model with a positive, but non-significant, relationship with performance is digital services (ß = 0.112, t = 1,258 and p > 0.05). The performance equation can then be written as :

PERÌ = 1110 - 0.106TÌ - 0.267SBPÌ + 0.112SDÌ + Di

The following table presents an overview of the relationship between SME performance and the quality of banking services in Jacmel, based on the results of the two models. This relationship can be interpreted through the signs and significance of the coefficients of the variables.

Tableau 6.   Overview of the relationship between SME performance and the quality banking services in Jacmel

Variable	Performance (CA)	Sig.	Performance (QCD)	Sig.
Interest rate		z		z
Payment services	+	z		Z
Digital services	+	z	+	z
Loan amount	+	z		
Loan term	+	z		

Sources: Authors' calculations based on 2023 data

In terms of QCD, payment banking services have a negative and significant impact on the performance of SMEs in Jacmel. The interest rate, although negatively correlated with performance, does not significantly influence it. Similarly, digital services, although positively correlated with performance, have no significant effect on it. In this context, hypothesis H2 is only partially validated.

At the same time, in terms of turnover, the interest rate behaves in the same way as in terms of QCD, i.e. it has a negative correlation with performance, but does not significantly affect it. The same applies to loan duration and payment services, which, contrary to expectations, show positive correlations with performance. On the other hand, it is the loan amount and digital services that have a positive and significant impact on performance. The result for digital services validates hypothesis H1.

The most likely reason for the positive effect of digital services on turnover is that, thanks to these improved services, SMEs can carry out transactions more easily and without having to resort to the traditional physical methods, which seem to present more complications for banks. This makes it easier for SMEs to buy and sell. Such services should therefore have a positive impact on the i'ierínrmance en terree de QCD Or ce n'eet пяе le ca"- ile ne cant nac significatifs. This could mean that companies need more than this to improve the quality and reduce the cost and time of the service they offer their customers in the market.

Conclusion

The aim of this study was to demonstrate that there is a relationship between the quality of banking services and the performance of SMEs in Jacmel, focusing on digital banking. Our aim was to fill a gap, as no previous study has analysed this relationship from such a broad perspective. Most studies on this subject focus mainly on a single aspect, namely financing, and do not seek to integrate other elements such as payment services or digital services. However, this was relevant, as many SMEs in Jacmel are experiencing banking malfunctions, particularly in relation to payment systems. It was therefore important to analyse the impact of these factors on the performance of local businesses, and especially the effect of digitisation, given the advantages it offers for improving the customer experience.

The only study in the literature that links banking digitalisation and SME performance is limited to online services. It does not take into account other important aspects, such as bank cards. Furthermore, it should be emphasised that performance has been understood in its commercial dimension, measured in terms of turnover and quality-cost-delivery time of SME products. As for the quality of banking services, this was approached from the angle of customer perception, implying the idea of satisfaction with these services.

We formulated two hypotheses to answer our research question: 1. digital banking has a positive effect on the turnover of SMEs in Jacmel; 2. digital banking has a positive effect on the quality-cost-delivery triptych of SMEs' products. Digital banking has a positive effect on the quality-cost-delivery time triptych for SME products. A questionnaire survey was carried out among 118 SMEs in the town. In principle, all of them are formal businesses, in that banks cannot have a normal relationship with them unless they are legally registered. These businesses operate in a variety of sectors and are spread throughout the city and its surrounding areas. The sampling method used combines a probability method and a reasoned choice method. In order to maximise the chances of obtaining a satisfactory response rate, the questionnaires were physically delivered to the owner-managers of the SMEs selected for data collection. Once collected, the data was processed and analysed using Excel and SPSS. Descriptive statistics and two multiple regression models were used for each performance measure.

The results show that, overall, all the explanatory variables selected, namely the interest rate, payment services and digital services, are correlated with performance, whether in terms of sales or quality - cost-delivery time for SMEs. However, significance varies according to the explanatory variable and its relationship with the variable being explained. The interest rate is negatively correlated with turnover and QCD, but is not significant. Payment services show a negative and significant correlation with QCD, while the correlation with turnover is positive, but not significant. As for digital services, they are positively correlated with turnover and QCD, but the correlation is significant with turnover and not significant with QCD. As a result, hypothesis H1 is fully validated, while hypothesis H2 is only partially validated.

The results show that, although the interest rate is relatively high, it does not prevent an increase in sales or reduce the quality, costs or delivery times of the SMEs' products. This is reflected in the beta coefficients observed. Payment services have no direct impact on turnover, as the vast majority of SMEs bypass these services by using other means to continue carrying out their transactions. However, these alternatives do influence product quality, costs and delivery times. As for digital services, although they do not have a direct impact on quality, costs and delivery times, they seem to be the only ones that are well perceived by businesses. The problem is that few of them use these services. This raises the question of the accessibility banking services.

The study has two main limitations. The first concerns the coefficients of determination of the models (R^2). Although they do not call into question the overall significance of the models (as confirmed by the Fisher tests), they are not sufficiently high. The most plausible explanation is that other control variables, apart from the amount and duration of the loan, were needed to explain performance. This seems all the more relevant given that company performance, in general, is influenced by a large number of factors.

The second limitation relates to the robustness of the models. Although standard tests have carried out and validated, it is possible that these models could be improved. However, even with new regressions, it is unlikely that the results will differ significantly when based on the quality of banking services as perceived by SME customers. This is why the study is so important for banks in terms of managerial involvement. It should enable them to gain a better understanding of how SME customers perceive their services, to improve payment services, which reduce quality and increase costs, as well as delivery times for SME products, and to strengthen the range of digital services, which appear to be beneficial for SMEs.

The contribution of the study, both theoretically and empirically, is therefore not negligible, especially in the Haitian context. What it uncovers paves the way for further research into other aspects of banking services, in relation the economy in general and business management in particular.

Bibliography

1   . Akitan, A. (2015). Bank financing and firm performance in Sub-Saharan Africa: Cases of Cameroon and Senegal. Laboratoire de Recherches économiques et Monetaires UCAD.

2   . Ambroise, G. (2019, March). Analysis of credit cycles and economic activity in Haiti. (BRH, Éd.) Cahier de Recherche (MAÉ/BRH-CR- 004), pp. 49-61.

3   . Bahia, K., & Nantel, J. (2000). A reliable and valid measurement scale for the perceived service quality of banks. International Journal of Bank Marketing, 28(2), 211-223.

4   . Bank of the Republic of Haiti. (2018). Rapport annuel.

5   . World Bank. (2020). Financial capability and inclusion in Haiti. Survey results.

6   . Barbot-Grizzo, M. C. (2012). Gestion et anticipation de la transmission des TPE

artisanales : vers une démarche proactive du dirigeant propriétaire. Management & Avenir, 2(52), 35-56.

7   . IDB. (2011). The Impact of Internet Banking on the Performance of Micro and Small Enterprises in Costa Rica: A Ramdomized Controlled Experiment. Working Papers (IDB-WP-242).

8   . Boyer, A., & Nefzi, A. (2009). La perception de la qualité dans le domaine des services : vers une clarification des concepts. La Revue des Sciences de Gestion, 3-4 (237-238), 43-54.

9   . International Labour Office. (2015). Small and medium-sized enterprises and the creation of decent and productive employment. International Labour Conference.

10 Cadet, L. R., Providence, C., & Antenord, J.-B. (2018). Banking Penetration and the Development of Haiti's Cities. In CREGED (Ed.), Accès aux biens et services en Haiti - Banque et Développement, (pp. 89-100). Port-au-Prince.

11 Doura, F. (2012). Economie d'Haiti, dépendance, crises et développement tome 2. Montreal, Canada: Les Editions DAMI.

12 Driss, E. (2017). Quality and business performance. Revue Marocaine de Recherche en Management et Marketing (16), 438-459.

13 .El Manzani, N., Asli, A., & El Manzani, Y. (2018). Factors of entrepreneurial failure in Moroccan SMEs: an exploratory study. Marché et Organisations, 3(33), 105-144.

14 Elouahabi, T., & Dakkon, M. (2022). La digitalisation bancaire: approche conceptuelle et théorique. International Journal of Accounting, Finance, Auditing, Management & Economics, 3(5-1), 199-210.

15 Etogo-Nyaga, Y. P. (2020). Access to finance and performance of SMEs in Cameroon. Revue " Repères et Perspectives économiques ", 4(1), 1-18.

16 Hafiane, M. A., & Jed, I. (2021). The impact of online banking quality on customer loyalty: A study through the mediating effect of the level of satisfaction of Moroccan customers. International Journal of Business and Technologies Studies and Research, 3(2).

17 IFC-World Bank. (2010). SME Banking Guide. Washington DC.

18 Issor, Z. (2017). Corporate performance: a complex concept with multiple dimensions. Projectique, 2(17), 93-103.

19 Lamaute-Brisson, N. (2002). The informal economy in Haiti. De la reproduction urbaine à Port-au-Prince. Paris: L'Harmattan.

20 Kone, B., & Thera, S. (2022). Impact de l'endettement sur la performance dans les PME du district de Bamako : Cas des BTP. International Journal of Economics and Management, 2(1).

21 Lakhrif, K., Faical, Z., & El Haddou, Y. (2016). The impact perceived service quality on the satisfaction and commitment of major customers: Cas de la Banque populaire marocaine. Recherches & Pratiques en Marketing, 1(1), 1-29.

22 Department of Trade and Industry. (2014). Business Census 2012-2013.

23 OECD. (2004). Promoting SMEs for Development. Characteristics and

Importance of SMEs, 2 (5), OECD Publishing, 37-46.

24 Paul, B., Juma'h, H. A., & Dorante, F. (2018). Entrepreneurs' Perception of Banks' Social Responsibility: A Haitian Case Study. In CREGED (Ed.), Accès aux biens et services en Haiti - Banque et Developpement, (pp. 7988). Port-au-Prince.

25 Sangue-Fotso, R., & Wamba, H. (2017). Perception of performance by their managers: The case of Cameroonian SMEs. Question(s) de Management (18), 155-171.

26 Tioumagneng, A. (2011). Bank credit maturities and firm performance: the case of Cameroon. Mondes en Développement (153), 7186.

27 Tsapi, V. (2020). The perception of service quality and the commitment of bank customers in Cameroon. Revue internationale des Sciences de Gestion, 3 (2).

28 Zeithmal, V. A. (1988). Consumer perceptions of price, quality and value: A means-end model and synthesis of evidence. Journal of Marketing, 52, 2-22.

Public choice and adoption of mobile money for financial inclusion in Haiti
Dr Christophe PROVIDENCE
Lecturer, Researcher at the CRS-IUS in Haiti.

Introduction

Financial inclusion is an essential component of economic development, particularly in countries where a large proportion of the population remains outside traditional banking systems (United States Agency for International Development, 2021). It represents an essential lever for economic development, especially in contexts where a large proportion of the population is excluded from traditional financial systems. In Haiti, where only around 30% of adults have a bank account, mobile money (such as MonCash) has emerged as an innovative solution to meet the needs of unbanked populations (World Bank Group, 2019).

Introduced as an innovative alternative, mobile money (MM) enables financial transactions to be carried out via a mobile phone, offering a potential solution to the challenges of financial inclusion. Since its introduction in Haiti in the post-earthquake context of 2010, mobile money has seen increasing adoption (United States Agency for International Development, 2021).

However, the adoption of this technology is encountering significant obstacles, linked to coordination between players, infrastructure shortcomings and user mistrust.

This study explores the impact of mobile money on financial inclusion in Haiti using the theory incompatible public choices developed by Christophe Providence (Providence, 2022). This theory emphasises that misalignments between the objectives of public and private actors, combined with structural constraints, can lead to inefficiencies in the implementation of public policies. By analysing these dynamics, we identify opportunities to overcome existing challenges and maximise the benefits of mobile money.

Firstly, incompatibility of public choices often results from the divergent priorities of the actors involved in a policy (Providence, 2022). In the case of the adoption of mobile money in Haiti, this problem of coordination between actors is evident in their specific objectives. For example, telecoms operators are looking to maximise profits and expand their customer base. They also rely on technological innovation to develop new products. In the case of public institutions, the aim is not only to promote financial inclusion in order to reduce economic inequality, but above all to put in place regulations to protect consumers. The stated aims of NGOs and international institutions are socio-economic development (Providence, 2020) greater financial inclusion and the eradication poverty through accessible tools such as mobile money (World Bank Group, 2019).

The conflict identified in this study stems from the strategic choices made by the primary players. Telecom operators may prioritise more profitable urban areas, while public institutions wish to favour rural areas where the need for financial inclusion is more pressing. This misalignment can create gaps in the geographical coverage of mobile money services.

Secondly, the theory points out that the absence of a centralised authority or a clear collaborative framework leads to fragmentation of effort (Providence, 2022). In Haiti, several players are involved in the mobile money ecosystem:

Multiple roles for telecoms operators (such as Digicel with MonCash): they provide the digital infrastructure, but also take on the role of educating users and managing agents.

Intervention by public authorities: often limited to regulating services, with no real logistical support or infrastructure!

Role of NGOs and international donors: complementary, but their projects are often one-off and targeted at specific communities.

Poorly defined roles lead to overlapping responsibilities or gaps in policy implementation. For example, user education can be neglected if no one actor takes full responsibility for it (United States Agency for International Development, 2021).

Finally, the theory of incompatible public choices highlights the importance of clear and coherent regulation to arbitrate the priorities of the various stakeholders (Providence, 2022). In Haiti, the regulatory challenges include

Lack of interoperability: Mobile money services in Haiti are often compartmentalised, preventing transfers between different operator networks. This limits the adoption and use of services. Insufficient user protection: The absence of strict regulations can expose users to hidden charges or the risk of fraud. Weak supervision of local agents: Local agents are not always well supervised, which can undermine the quality services and customer confidence.

Public authorities lack the means to impose binding rules on operators, while the latter favour solutions that maximise their control over the ecosystem.

After outlining the quality of the data in this study (I), a theoretical position is needed to justify the relevance of financial inclusion for Haiti (II). Thus, an initial analysis of the impact of mobile money on financial inclusion in Haiti (III) followed by an analysis of the current digital divide (IV) and the implementation of a national plan to combat it (V).

I- Field methodology for capturing financial inclusion

The adoption of mobile money in Haiti offers immense potential for financial inclusion, but requires better coordination and strategic integration of efforts (Aker & Mbiti, 2010). By overcoming the institutional misalignments identified by the Christophe Providence (2022) theory, it would be possible to increase the reach, efficiency and sustainability of digital financial services. Cross-sector collaboration, supported by inclusive public policies, is essential to turn these challenges into opportunities.

1- The data collection process

The study uses a mixed approach combining qualitative and quantitative analysis to examine the impact of mobile money on financial inclusion:

a) *Data collection for the Mémoire de Mo'ise Masson in 2024*

- User survey: 313 respondents from zones

urban and rural areas were questioned about their adoption, perception and use of mobile money services.

• Qualitative interviews: in-depth discussions with operators telecoms (such as Digicel), government representatives and NGOs involved in promoting financial inclusion.

• Secondary data: National statistics on financial inclusion and reports from the Central Bank of Haiti.

b) *Data analysis*

• Statistical analysis: Regressions to identify the determinants of 1 adoption of mobile money (age, income, level of education, etc.).

• Theoretical framework: Application of the Christophe Providence theory to understand institutional and structural misalignments.

c) Case studies

• Specific example: implementation of MonCash as a platform of mobile money in Haiti.

This dual data collection method made it possible to reach a wide range of populations, including poorly connected rural areas. The variables were divided into two main categories:

• **Socio-economic characteristics**: age, level of education, income, occupation, gender.

• **Perceived usefulness**: ease of use, time savings, security, distance from physical banks.

To facilitate the analysis, the following 3 figures are used.

a) Representation of banks available in different zones geographical ;

b) Growth in the percentage mobile phone users in Haiti from 2010 to 2020 :

c) Growth of mobile money in Haiti from 2010 to 2020

Figure 1 could represent a network coverage map, a comparison of urban and rural areas, or an assessment access to mobile money.

If Figure 1 shows a geographical breakdown, it is likely that urban areas have denser coverage than rural areas. This illustrates the structural challenge of the digital divide, requiring telecoms infrastructure to be extended to remote areas. The challenge now is to identify the regions that benefit from better access and those that are underserved. Remote rural areas could be the hardest hit by the lack of infrastructure, for example. Public policy would be to prioritise investment in underserved areas improve digital inclusion.

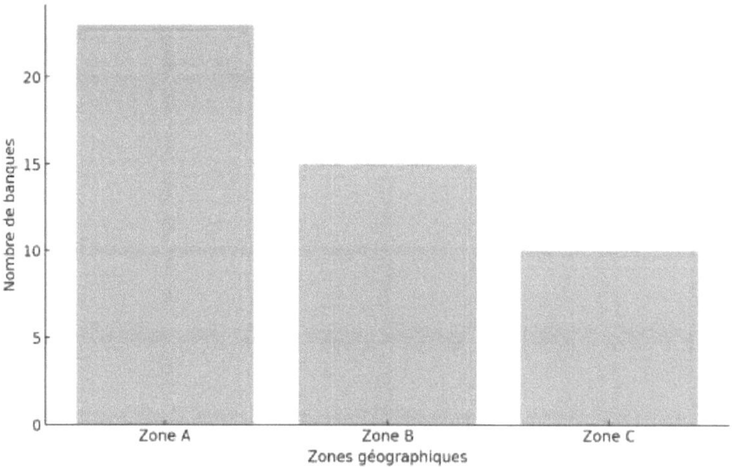

Source: Data from the Moise Masson survey in 2024

Figure 2 could present an analysis of adoption rates by age, gender, income or geographical region. On the one hand, young urban dwellers could represent the majority of users, thanks to better access to smartphones and connectivity. As a result, middle- and high-income brackets could show a higher adoption rate. On the other hand, rural populations, women and the elderly may show limited adoption, linked to barriers such as digital literacy or high costs.

The recommendations would be :

•   Develop targeted awareness campaigns for at-risk groups.
low uptake ;

•   Offering appropriate solutions, such as basic telephones or simplified interfaces.

Figure 2: Number of mobile phone users (%)

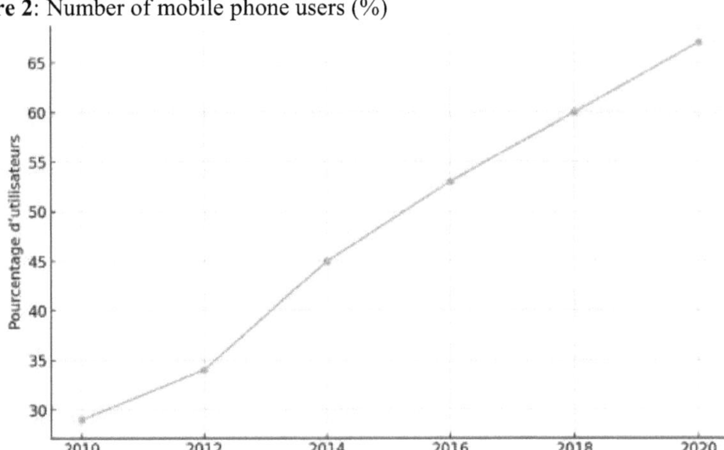

Source: Data from the Moise Masson survey in 2024

Figure 3 could show an increase in transactions, money or access to credit thanks to mobile money. If transactions are increasing over time, this indicates that mobile money is meeting a growing need for financial services. An upward trend could also indicate increased user confidence.

Urban populations or micro-entrepreneurs could be the main beneficiaries, while farmers or rural populations are less represented. Hence the need broaden the range of services on offer to include financial products tailored specific needs, such as microcredit for farmers.

Figure 3: Growth of mobile money in Haiti between 2010 and 2020

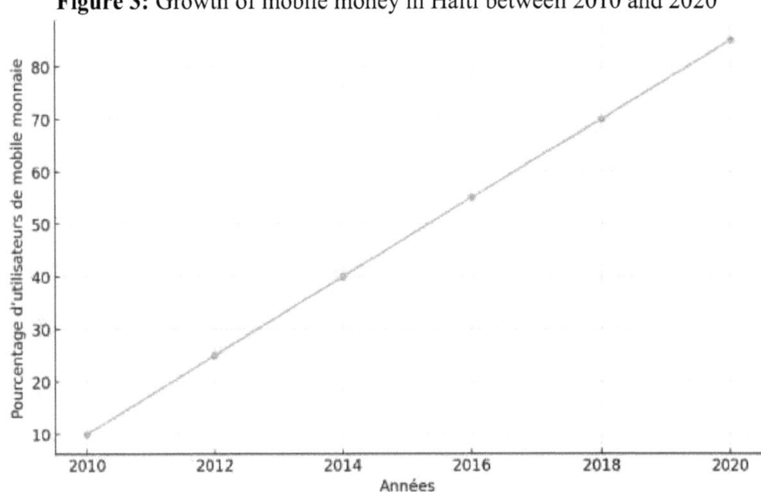

Source: Data from the Moise Masson survey in 2024

Figures 4, 5 and 6 provide key insights into the state of infrastructure, adoption rates and impact of mobile money in Haiti. In-depth analysis reveals significant disparities between demographic and geographic groups, highlighting priority areas for intervention.

2- *The challenge of coordinating players*

The lack of coordination between telecoms operators, public authorities and financial institutions creates structural inefficiencies and is the primary concern of this study. It can be seen that operators prioritise urban areas for reasons of profitability, while public policies seek to extend coverage in rural areas (Providence, 2022).

These incompatible choices result a divergence of interests: profit maximisation for private operators versus social objectives for public players. The result is :

- Weak coverage in rural areas, leaving a large part of the
excluded population.
- Multiplication of isolated efforts by NGOs and institutions
without strategic alignment.

The second concern relates to the fragmentation of roles and responsibilities. In this case, telecoms operators take on several roles (infrastructure providers, user education, agent management), leading to overload and gaps in certain critical areas. The financial education of users, often delegated to agents, is inadequate due to a lack of specialist training. Also, the fragmentation of responsibilities reflects a lack of systemic planning and a common vision, exacerbated by budgetary and institutional constraints. Users, particularly in rural areas, are unfamiliar with the services or reluctant to use them for fear of fraud or hidden costs.

It is easy to see the tensions in the allocation of resources that justify the third concern of this study. It shows that available resources are concentrated in one-off or redundant initiatives, with no real strategic integration. Operators invest in costly advertising campaigns to attract customers, but neglect the development of sustainable infrastructure in remote areas. These tensions illustrate a lack of collective prioritisation, with each player pursuing its own objectives without assessing their compatibility with the long-term needs of the ecosystem. As a result, there are persistent imbalances between urban and rural areas, exacerbating economic and financial inequalities.

The last concern leads to consideration of the problems of user confidence. Mistrust of mobile money systems stems from frequent cases of fraud, a lack of transparency on charges and low awareness. Many users share their PIN with agents or friends at , increasing the risk of unauthorised access (United States Agency for International Development, 2021). User confidence is compromised by the lack of a coherent consumer protection structure, a problem amplified by the misalignment of stakeholder priorities. The result is limited take-up of mobile money services, particularly for complex transactions such savings or credit.

Applying Christophe Providence's theory, this analysis reveals that the challenges to the adoption of mobile money in Haiti are not just technical, but profoundly institutional and structured. The incompatible choices made by stakeholders (operators, government, NGOs) amplify inefficiencies and slow progress towards equitable financial inclusion.

II- Theoretical basis for financial inclusion in Haiti

In addition to Christophe Providence's (2022) theory of incompatible public choices, other theoretical models can be applied to analyse the adoption of mobile money and its impact on financial inclusion in Haiti. These models offer additional perspectives on the interactions between actors, structures and users.

1- *Theories that can be used to understand ¡financial inclusion*

The Diffusion of Innovation theory (Rogers, 2003) offers an interesting analytical framework. This theory explains how, why and at what rate an innovation (such as mobile money) spreads through a society. Users are categorised as: innovators, early adopters, early majority, late majority, and laggards.

In Haiti, young urban people, who are better educated and have access to technology, are the early adopters of mobile money. They often influence rural and marginalised communities to try these services. However, there are two barriers for the late majority and late adopters: low digital literacy and mistrust of digital financial systems.

Another theory (Van Dijk, 2006) also lends itself to the analysis of financial inclusion in Haiti. This theory explores the gaps between groups that have equitable access to digital technologies and those that do not, due to socio-economic, geographical or cultural factors. Consider the "urban-rural" divide, which explains why rural areas suffer from limited access to telecoms infrastructure, reducing their take-up of mobile money. The economic divide must also be taken into account: low-income households are reluctant to adopt these services because of the transaction costs.

Capability theory (Sen, 2001) emphasises the development of individual freedoms and capabilities to enable people to fulfil their potential. Digital financial services, such as mobile money, are seen as tools for improving economic and social freedoms. To build economic capacity in Haiti, mobile money facilitates access to credit, savings and remittances, improving people's ability to manage their finances. However, obstacles such as lack of education or cultural barriers limit access to these services.

The theory of Network Extemalities offers a relevant framework for analysis (Katz & Shapiro, 1985). This theory postulates that the value of a service increases with the number of people who use it. Services such as mobile money become more useful and attractive when more people, merchants and institutions adopt them. In Haiti, there is a need to strengthen this network by encouraging small traders, farmers and micro-entrepreneurs to integrate mobile money into their transactions. Urban agents and users can influence rural areas by demonstrating the benefits of digital services. To act effectively, two solutions could be adopted:

• Offer financial incentives to retailers and local institutions
to promote the use of mobile money;

• Strengthen interoperability between different operators to
increase the perceived usefulness of the network.

In the context of this study, the TAM (Technology Acceptance Model) may be of interest (Davis, 1989). This model examines the factors that influence the adoption of a technology, mainly :

• Perceived usefulness: The degree to which a technology is perceived as being useful.

beneficial.

• Perceived ease of use: The degree to which the technology is perceived as easy to use.

For an application in Haiti, there are barriers to overcome. The first relates to perceived usefulness (rural users may not see the immediate benefits of mobile money services) and the second to ease of use (complex menus and lack of digital literacy hinder adoption).

Game theory can be used to enrich this analysis financial inclusion in Haiti (Osborne & Rubinstein, 1994). This theory explores the strategic interactions between the various players, modelling their decisions to maximise their gains. In the context of mobile money, the players include telecoms operators, banks, the government and users. To do this, we need to take into account not only competition between operators (operators are reluctant to collaborate in order to protect their customer base), but also the interaction between public and private players (misalignments in "profit vs. social inclusion" objectives can lead to inefficiencies).

Finally, the theory of innovation ecosystems interesting analytical perspectives for Haiti (Moore, 1996). This theory views innovation as a dynamic system in which interconnected actors work together to create value. It focuses on the relationships between companies, public institutions, users and technology providers. In Haiti, we can look at the lack of synergy between players, for example. NGOs, telecoms operators and public institutions often work in silos, limiting overall impact.

These models offer various perspectives for analysing and improving the adoption of mobile money in Haiti. A multidimensional approach, integrating Diffusion of Innovation theory, TAM, and Game theory, could help overcome the current challenges. By aligning the interests of stakeholders and putting the user at the centre of efforts, it would be possible to accelerate financial inclusion while responding to local specificities.

2- *A few examples (¡financial inclusion in the world*

The following are international examples of projects that have succeeded in strengthening financial inclusion through digital technology, thanks to coordinated, multi-sector initiatives. These experiences may inspire the implementation of a national plan in Haiti.

a) Kenya: M-Pesa and ¡financial inclusion

In 2007, Safaricom launched M-Pesa, a mobile money platform, in a country where the majority of the population was unbanked.

Actions implemented

1. Cross-sector collaboration :

- Safaricom has worked   with with NGOS,   NGOs,   local banks and   the
government to promote the adoption of M-Pesa ;
- Forming networks of local agents to offer services
accessible, even in rural areas.
2. Adapted technology :
- Use of the USSD system, available on basic phones ;
- Development of interoperability between banks and M-Pesa in order to
expand financial services.
3. User education :
- Awareness-raising campaigns in local languages to explain the
advantages of mobile money.

Results obtained :

96% of Kenyan households now have access to M-Pesa.

Improved financial inclusion, with a direct impact on poverty reduction.

Women and farmers have been able to access microcredit and savings tools.

b) Bangladesh: Mobile money with bKash

bKash, launched in 2011, has democratised digital financial services in a country where less than 15% of the population has a bank account.

Actions implemented

1. Extensive network of agents :
- Training thousands staff to provide local services, even in the most remote areas.
in the most remote areas.
2. Partnership with banks :
- Working with banks to manage funds and ensure security
transactions.
3. Targeted campaigns:
- Raising awareness of the use of services via television advertising
and community sessions.

Results obtained

- Over 50% of the population use bKash for money transfers,
bill payments and savings.
- Increased economic opportunities thanks to access to
digital financial services.

c) Estonia: e-Estonia (digHalisanon of public services)

Estonia has digitised all its public services to guarantee universal access for its citizens.

Actions implemented

1. National digital platform :
- Setting up a centralised platform manage interactions
between citizens and institutions.
2. Training and awareness :

- Compulsory digital training in schools to ensure that every citizen is digitally literate.

3. Digital identity :

- Providing digital identities secure access to services.

Results obtained :

- Over 99% of public services available online.

- Accelerating the adoption of digital tools by the whole workforce population.

These examples show that bridging the digital divide requires a combination robust infrastructure, strategic partnerships and educational efforts. As a result, financial inclusion requires investment in rural infrastructure, cross-sector collaboration to train networks of local agents and the adoption of lightweight solutions. Haiti can draw on these experiences to solutions adapted to its local context, prioritising rural areas and vulnerable populations.

• II- Impacts of mobile money on financial inclusion in Haiti

The adoption of mobile money has a significant impact on financial inclusion in Haiti, offering opportunities to overcome the limitations of traditional banking systems and fostering better integration of marginalised populations into the financial ecosystem (United States Agency for International Development, 2021). There are several dimensions to these impacts.

1- Implementation of ¡financial inclusion in Haiti

Mobile money gives unbanked people, particularly those living in rural and remote areas, access to essential financial services. Users can open a mobile money account simply with a mobile phone, without the need for a physical bank branch. In Haiti, where less than 30% of adults have a bank account, mobile money is becoming a key solution to fill this gap (World Bank Group, 2019).

Mobile money also reduces the cost using financial services compared with traditional banks. Charges for deposits and transfers via mobile money are often lower than those charged by banks. This means that low-income populations can access these services without incurring the prohibitive costs of traditional financial institutions.

By introducing simple financial tools, mobile money encourages a better understanding of financial services. Mobile money agents often educate users on how to manage their transactions. This contributes to a gradual improvement in financial literacy in areas where formal education is limited.

Mobile money is helping to reduce the gender gap in access to financial services. Women, who often face barriers in accessing traditional banking services, can use mobile money to save, receive payments or manage funds. This strengthens women's economic independence and contributes to their empowerment.

In practice, mobile money simplifies transactions for micro-entrepreneurs and small businesses, encouraging their development. Local merchants can receive digital payments and avoid handling large sums of cash, thereby reducing the risk of fraud.

This improves their access to customers, even in remote areas, and facilitates their integration into formal value chains.

Mobile money offers a secure and rapid alternative for transferring funds in times of crisis. During the 2010 earthquake, for example, mobile money platforms played a key role in the rapid distribution of humanitarian aid. Vulnerable households can receive emergency funds instantly, boosting their ability to cope with economic shocks.

Mobile money services extend their coverage to regions where there is no banking infrastructure. By using local agents, mobile money platforms offer financial services in areas where banks are not present. This helps to reduce the "rural-urban" gap in access to financial services.

Mobile money simplifies and speeds up domestic and international remittances. Haitians in the diaspora can transfer money directly to the mobile wallets of their loved ones. Households benefit from fast, secure transfers, often at lower cost, increasing their purchasing power.

Mobile money platforms allow users to store money securely and develop savings habits. Apps offer automated savings options or dedicated savings accounts. This encourages long-term financial planning, particularly for low-income households.

By making financial services more accessible, mobile money reduces inequalities in access between rich and poor populations. Marginalised populations, often excluded from traditional banks, can use mobile money to manage their finances. This helps to reduce economic disparities and strengthen social cohesion.

Despite these positive impacts, certain challenges still limit the potential of mobile money for financial inclusion:

Costs are still high for certain transactions (withdrawals, international transfers).

Low digital literacy in rural areas ;

Lack of trust in digital systems due to security and confidentiality concerns;

Uneven coverage by local agents, leaving some rural areas underserved.

Mobile money represents a major step forward for financial inclusion in Haiti. It fills the gaps left by traditional banking systems, while offering innovative solutions for savings, money transfers and access to credit. By overcoming the current challenges through appropriate policies and strategic partnerships, mobile money could bring about a lasting transformation of the Haitian economy by including marginalised populations in the financial system.

2- *The issue of interoperabilityfinanciers*

Financial interoperability, i.e. the ability of different payment systems and financial platforms to work together seamlessly, is essential to maximise the impact of mobile money services and promote financial inclusion. In Haiti, this interoperability faces several major challenges.

Local regulations do not always set clear standards to force or encourage operators to make their systems interoperable. Each operator (for example, Digicel with MonCash) maintains closed platforms, preventing users from transferring money between different services (Digicel Haiti, 2022). Specific regulations will need to be put in place to encourage interoperability, while ensuring a balance between competition and collaboration.

Telecoms operators see interoperability as a threat to their competitiveness, as it could make it easier for customers to switch from one service to another. They prefer closed solutions to retain their users, thus limiting the expansion of interoperable services. It would be wise encourage operators to adopt revenue-sharing models to offset the fear of losing customers.

Interoperability robust, shared technical infrastructures, such as common clearing systems and payment gateways. In the absence of such infrastructures, each operator invests in its own systems, creating isolated technological islands. The BRH (like the country's central bank) could develop a centralised interoperable national platform, managed by a neutral authority.

Implementing interoperability requires significant initial investment to adapt existing systems and guarantee their compatibility. The high costs involved are holding back the willingness of operators and financial institutions to commit to this transition. The State could provide subsidies or tax incentives to offset the implementation costs for operators.

End-users, particularly in rural areas, often have little confidence in digital systems, which hinders their adoption of interoperable services. Interoperability efforts not reach their full potential if users are reluctant to carry out transactions between systems. Awareness campaigns could be launched to explain the benefits of interoperability and build user confidence.

There is also the problem of agent network fragmentation. Mobile money agents generally work for a single operator, limiting their ability to offer interoperable services. As a result, customers have to go to specific points of service to carry out transactions, which limits their convenience. Agents will need to be trained and authorised to manage multiple platforms, enabling them to process interoperable transactions.

Furthermore, interoperability between different systems increases the points of entry for cyber attacks and fraud, complicating security management. Operators fear a deterioration in their reputation in the event of security breaches in interconnected systems. It is up to the public authorities to adopt common security standards and strengthen collaboration between operators to prevent incidents.

A large proportion of the Haitian population, particularly in rural areas, has a poor understanding of financial and digital concepts. Users can be confused by interoperability and have difficulty navigating between different systems. Hence the need to launch digital and financial education campaigns to help users take full advantage of interoperable services.

Admittedly, some traditional banks see interoperability as a threat to their business model, fearing that they will lose their central role in the financial system. Their resistance could slow down the integration of banking services with mobile money platforms. However, banks still need to be involved in the design of interoperability as essential partners.

Finally, the Haitian government and the Central Bank sometimes lack the resources and technical skills needed to steer a large-scale interoperability project. The lack of leadership slows down coordination between the players. Institutional capacity should be strengthened through support from international organisations and public-private partnerships.

Financial interoperability is an essential condition for maximising the impact of mobile money services on financial inclusion in Haiti. However, the challenges identified require a collaborative and progressive approach:

1. Adopt incentive-based regulation (the Central Bank must
interoperability while guaranteeing a competitive framework);

2. Create a shared national platform (an infrastructure
(e.g. a central database, managed by a neutral entity, to simplify interoperable transactions);

3. Provide financial incentives (encourage operators to collaborate by offsetting part of the implementation costs);

4. Raising awareness among users (launching awareness campaigns)
communication on the benefits of interoperability) ;

5. Involve all stakeholders (banks, operators, NGOs, etc.) in the process.
and government must be aligned on common objectives).

Interoperability not only makes financial services more accessible, it also strengthens confidence in digital systems, paving the way for a genuine economic transformation in Haiti.

IV- Bridging the digital divide in Haiti: Strategies and recommendations

The digital divide, defined as the gap in access to and use of digital technologies between different socio-economic, geographical or demographic groups, is a major obstacle to economic and social development. In Haiti, this divide is exacerbated by structural challenges such as limited access to electricity, poor network coverage and low levels literacy. Here are some concrete strategies for reducing this divide.

1. Improving ¡digital infrastructure

The first problem to be resolved is the poor coverage of telecoms networks in rural areas and limited access to electricity, which hampers the use of digital technologies. Possible solutions would be :

a) Expansion of mobile networks (invest in the installation of telecom towers in rural areas and encourage operators to use low-cost technologiessuch as fixed 4G or satellite networks);

b) Off-grid electrification (promoting solar solutions and microgrids in rural areas to energy to households and telecoms infrastructures);

c) Public-private partnerships (encourage collaboration between government, telecoms operators and international organisations to share costs and risks).

A second problem relates to the cost of access to technologies. For example, the high cost of smartphones, mobile data and digital services limits their adoption by low-income households.

Possible solutions would be :

a)   Subsidies for smartphones (launch subsidy programmes to make smartphones accessible at a reduced price and encourage the import and distribution of basic phones compatible with USSD services);

b)   Affordable data packages (introduce mobile data packages specially designed for rural and low-income populations and promote lightweight applications that require little data to operate);

c)   Eliminating taxes (reducing or eliminating taxes on ICT equipment to reduce their cost).

digital and financial literacy is the third issue to be considered. In reality, it is the low level understanding of digital technologies and financial services among rural and uneducated populations.

Possible solutions would be :

a)   Digital education (integrating digital training courses into schools and community centres and organising practical workshops to learn how to use smartphones, mobile money applications and other digital tools);

b)   Awareness campaigns in Creole (teaching materials and educational videos in Haitian Creole to reach local populations):

c)   Training local agents (building the capacity of mobile money agents to act as educators in their communities).

A fourth problem is the lack of interoperability between digital systems. It is essential avoid compartmentalisation of digital services, which limits their usefulness to end users. The challenge is to improve the usefulness of digital technologies, thereby increasing their adoption by users.

Possible solutions would be :

a)   Interoperability between telecom operators (enabling transfers between different mobile money platforms, such as MonCash and NatCash);

b)   Standardisation of platforms (create a common platform managed by a neutral entity to centralise digital transactions);

c)   Collaboration between institutions (promoting partnerships between banks, telecoms operators and fintech providers to offer integrated services).

The lack of economic incentives for digital adoption is a fifth issue to be addressed. For example, rural and disadvantaged populations do not always see the immediate benefits of digital technologies.

Possible solutions would be :

a.   Incentive programmes (offering rewards to new users such as free credits for the first mobile money transactions);

b.   Grants for SMEs (provide funding help micro-businesses integrate digital tools into their activities);

c. Mobile agent networks extend mobile agent networks to enable users to access digital services easily).

A sixth problem stems from ineffective public policy and regulation. There is even a lack of clear policies to coordinate efforts to reduce the digital divide in Haiti.

Possible solutions would be :

a) National plan for the digital divide (develop a national strategy with measurable objectives to reduce the digital divide) ;

b) Regulation of operators (imposing universal coverage obligations on telecoms operators) ;

c) International collaboration (seeking help   from   organisations
to initiate and support programmes to reduce the digital divide).

In short, reducing the digital divide in Haiti requires a holistic approach, combining investment in infrastructure, appropriate educational programmes and targeted economic incentives. By simultaneously tackling the technological, economic and cultural barriers, it is possible to transform the digital divide into a development opportunity, while accelerating social and financial inclusion.

V- Implementation of a national plan to reduce the digital divide in Haiti

Implementing a national plan requires a systematic and inclusive approach, involving the government, telecoms operators, financial institutions, NGOs and international organisations. Here is a detailed framework for designing and implementing such a plan.

1. *The planning stage enables :*

a. Identify clear primary objectives (reducing the gap in access to digital technologies between urban and rural areas; promoting social and financial inclusion through digitisation) and specific objectives (increasing network coverage to 90% of rural areas within 5 years; doubling digital literacy rate among vulnerable populations; reducing the cost of digital equipment for low-income households by 50%);

b. Assess the current situation in terms of infrastructure (identify regions without network or electricity coverage), needs (assess the level digital literacy and access to digital services) and stakeholders (list the players involved, such as the government, telecoms operators, NGOs and donors);

c. Develop a national strategy (draw up a strategic framework defining priorities, performance indicators and the necessary resources) with strategic components (digital infrastructure, financial accessibility and digital literacy and awareness).

2. *The mobilisation of the preñantes parties presupposes :*

Coordinating public players (leading initiatives, policies and ensuring regulation), telecoms operators and access providers (extending networks and offering affordable services) and NGOs and international organisations (providing technical expertise, funding and field programmes) through public-private partnerships (creating a framework for cross-sector collaboration to share costs and risks. For example, the government finances rural infrastructure, while operators provide maintenance) while relying on community participation (involving local leaders and community representatives in the design and implementation of projects to ensure their relevance and acceptance).

3. Operational implementation requires :

a. Infrastructure development (installing cell towers in unserved areas; using alternative solutions such as satellite networks or fixed 4G for areas) and rural electrification (setting up microgrids and solar systems to power infrastructure and users);

b. Financial accessibility through equipment subsidies (subsidising smartphones or offering basic phones adapted to USSD services) and reduced access costs (offering low-cost mobile data packages in rural areas);

c. Training and awareness-raising based on digital literacy (setting up digital education programmes in schools, community centres and via mobile agents) and awareness-raising campaigns (using local media [radio, posters, social networks] to promote the benefits of digitisation).

4. The creation of a regulatory and incentive framework

a. Regulation of operators by promoting a universal coverage obligation (requiring operators to cover a minimum percentage of rural areas) and interoperability (making it compulsory for mobile money services and other digital platforms to be compatible);

b. Tax incentives (offering tax exemptions or subsidies for companies investing in rural infrastructure) ;

c. Consumer protection (introduce laws to ensure transparency of charges and security of user data).

5. The monitoring and evaluation system

a. Progress monitoring (set up a real-time monitoring system to assess the progress of initiatives such as infrastructure deployed, users reached, etc.);

b. Key performance indicators (percentage of network coverage; rate of use of digital services in rural areas; reduction in the average cost of access to technologies).

c. Periodic evaluations (independent audits every 6 months to identify obstacles and adjust strategies).

6. Communication and promotion

a. Sharing successes (documenting and sharing positive results to motivate stakeholders and attract new partners);

b. Maintain a public dialogue (organise regular forums between the government, communities and private stakeholders to ensure transparency and ongoing adaptation).

Concrete example: Plan for rural Haiti

1. Phase 1 (0-2 years) :
- Mapping priority needs.
- Install basic infrastructure (mobile networks, solar energy).
- Launch pilot digital education programmes.
2. Phase 2 (2-5 years) :

- Extending infrastructure to the remaining areas.
- Offer grants to equip schools and centres
community.
- Introduce mandatory interoperability between operators.
3. Phase 3 (5-10 years) :
- Assess the overall impact and adjust policies accordingly.
- Integrate digital services into all key sectors (education,
agriculture, trade).

Implementing a national plan to reduce the digital divide in Haiti is an ambitious process, but one that is essential for stimulating social and economic inclusion. By following a structured and collaborative approach, the country can not only reduce digital inequalities, but also create the conditions for sustainable and equitable development.

Conclusion

Mobile money represents a major step forward for financial inclusion in Haiti. It fills the gaps left by traditional banking systems, while offering innovative solutions for savings, money transfers and access to credit. By overcoming the current challenges through appropriate policies and strategic partnerships, mobile money could bring about a lasting transformation of the Haitian economy by including marginalised populations in the financial system.

Providence theory highlights the challenges of allocating resources in an environment where they are limited. In Haiti, allocation choices in the mobile money ecosystem raise complex questions:

- Investment in rural areas (telecoms operators can
hesitate to invest in the costly infrastructure needed to reach rural areas, for fear of immediate profitability);
- Subsidising services (public authorities may wish to
subsidise the cost access to mobile money for vulnerable populations, while operators seek to maintain their profitability);
- Staff training (resources allocated to staff training)
may be insufficient if operators, NGOs and governments do not agree on their funding).

Implementing a national plan to reduce the digital divide in Haiti is an ambitious process, but one that is essential stimulating social and economic inclusion. By following a structured and collaborative approach, the country can not only reduce digital inequalities, but also create the conditions for sustainable and equitable development. Involving these stakeholders in a coordinated way ensures that efforts to reduce the digital divide in Haiti will be sustainable and inclusive. Each party makes an essential contribution, whether in terms of funding, technology or community mobilisation. Success depends on close collaboration and a clear division of responsibilities.

The involvement of local communities is essential to ensure the success and sustainability of initiatives aimed at reducing the digital divide. By involving local people in the process, projects become more relevant, accepted and sustainable. What's more, by adopting an inclusive, participatory approach that is adapted to local needs, digital projects can gain in relevance and impact. These efforts must be part of a long-term vision, in which local populations become both beneficiaries and agents of change.

Bibliography

1. Aker, J., & Mbiti, I. M. (2010). Mobile Phones and Economic Development in Africa. *Journal of Economic Perspectives*, 207-232.

2. Davis, F. D. (1989). Perceived Usefulness, Perceived Ease of Use, and User Acceptance of Information Technology. *MIS Quarterly*, 319-340.

3. Digicel Haiti. (2022). *MonCash Annual Report.* Port-au-Prince: Digicel Haiti.

4. World Bank Group. (2019). *Financial capability and inclusion in Haiti: Findings from a demand-side survey.* Washington: UKLAD.

5. Katz, M. L., & Shapiro, C. (1985). Network Externalities, Competition, and Compatibility. *The American Economic Review*, 424-440.

6. Moore, J. F. (1996). *The Death of Competition: Leadership and Strategy in the Age of Business Ecosystems.* New York: HarperBusiness.

7. Osborne, M. J., & Rubinstein, A. (1994). *A Course in Game Theory.* Cambridge: MIT Press.

8. Providence, C. (2020). Development aid in Haiti: paradoxical responses to territorial imbalances. *Nouvelles Perspectives en Sciences Sociales*, 181-216.

9. Providence, C. (2022). *The paradoxes of change in Haiti: Public policy and territorial development.* Pointe-à-Pitre: Presses de l'Université des Antilles.

10. Rogers, E. M. (2003). *Diffusion of innovations.* New York: The Free Press.

11. Sen, A. (2001). *Development as freedom.* Oxford: Oxford Up Elt.

12. United States Agency for International Development. (2021). *Accessible Finance Activity in Haiti.* Washington: The World Council/USAID.

13. Van Dijk, J. A. (2006). Digital divide: Research, achievements and shortcomings. *Poetics*, 221-235.

An Imbricative Approach to Evaluating the Effectiveness of Health Information Systems in Carrefour, Haiti

Mr Jerry Rood LUBIN
Research assistant at the CRS-IUS in Haiti.
Dr Christophe PROVIDENCE
Lecturer, Researcher at the CRS-IUS in Haiti.

Introduction

HISs are crucial tools for managing medical data in the healthcare sector. However, their deployment in low-resource contexts, such as the commune of Carrefour in Haiti, is often hampered by socio-economic and organisational factors. Nesting theory (Providence, 2022) highlights the dynamic interactions between three levels of analysis:

- Technical: Infrastructures and technological tools ;
- Social: End-users, their skills and attitudes ;
- Organisational: Policies, processes and structures.

This integrative approach enables us to understand how these dimensions interact to influence the effectiveness SIS.

Haiti faces many challenges in the health sector. Its complex geographical situation and limited access to resources exacerbate the difficulties of providing adequate care for the entire population. These constraints make improving the health system particularly difficult, due to the isolation of certain areas and disparities in access to services. The country remains one of the most vulnerable in the world to natural disasters, mainly hurricanes, floods and earthquakes (World Bank, 2024), which weakens the already inadequate health infrastructure. In the face of these challenges, health needs are only growing in a context where resources are already scarce.

Medical records management in the country often faces problems such as data loss, duplication of effort and difficulty in accessing critical medical information quickly. The lack of widespread adoption digital technologies in the Haitian healthcare also limits access to the potential benefits of telemedicine, electronic medical records and other Health 4.0 innovations (PAHO, 2024). Healthcare professionals and patients still face challenges such as limited access to centralised medical data, delays in the transmission of critical information, and gaps in nationwide disease monitoring.

The adoption and integration of health information systems remains uneven across the country, with marked differences between urban and rural areas. Carrefour, at $18^W32'$ north latitude and $72^W25'$ west longitude, is one of the country's largest urban communes, located in the metropolitan area of Port-au-Prince, the capital of Haiti. It presents a particularly interesting case for analysing the effectiveness HIS in a context where the challenges associated with urbanisation, population density and access to care are particularly pronounced (Medicai Record System, 2017; Providence, 2022). As a dynamic urban area, the municipality is faced with growing public health needs despite being distinguished by a concentration of healthcare facilities, including public and private hospitals and modest medical centres. This situation makes it an ideal site for assessing the effectiveness of health information systems in managing electronic medical records (EMRs) and their impact on the quality of care.

Given the fragile health infrastructure, optimising health information systems to manage medical records poses a number of challenges in terms of continuity of care, data protection and access to care. To what extent do the SISs in the Carrefour municipality meet local needs while adapting to social, technical and organisational challenges? How can the interweaving of these dimensions guide the improvement of practices?

The introduction and optimisation of HIS can potentially deliver significant improvements by streamlining processes, facilitating access to medical information and enhancing care coordination. Such integration could potentially transform the management of medical records, contributing to more efficient care delivery and better public health (Wurster, et al., 2024). To this end, three research objectives will be pursued:

1. Identify the specific challenges at each level (technical, social, organisational) ;
2. Evaluate their interconnections and their impact on EMR management;
3. Suggest solutions to optimise SIS.

This study proposes an in-depth evaluation the effectiveness of health information systems. It aims to explore current practices in the management of electronic medical records in the municipality of Carrefour, highlighting the dynamics, opportunities and possible innovations in the context of health information systems (HIS). It explores a number of dimensions, including the state of the technological infrastructure in place, local public policies, the level of skills healthcare staff and the implications for the accessibility, integrity and confidentiality of medical data (Medicai Record System, 2017; Providence, 2022). Using a modern, rigorous and contextualised approach, it aims to understand how these technological tools can be better integrated to meet the needs of health professionals and the population, while international norms and standards and local realities (Providence, 2022).

The study is based on a mixed approach combining analysis of practices in local healthcare establishments, surveys of the tools and methods used and comparison with similar systems in international contexts. The three sites studied are :

1. Hópital Adventiste d'Haiti (HAH): Use of systems such as Afga and FileMaker ;
2. Carrefour Hospital: Use of Otus CMS and Microsoft Access ;
3. Health and Wellness CLINIC: Predominance of Excel and paper archives.

This study evaluates (I) the effectiveness of Health Information Systems (HIS) for managing electronic medical records (EMR) in Haiti (II) and particularly in the commune of Carrefour (III). The results reveal major challenges linked to limited interoperability, the absence of a legal framework and insufficient technological infrastructure (IV). Strategic recommendations are put forward for improving HIS, in particular by adopting international standards, improving infrastructures and providing ongoing training for healthcare staff (V).

I. Setting up health information systems

Digitisation in hospitals and the healthcare sector as a whole is an important and much-discussed issue in healthcare policy.

An international comparison of digital health strategies, carried out by the Bertelsmann Foundation, showed that in Europe, Estonia, Spain and the UK are digitally advanced countries in terms of political activity (e.g. state funding), preparation for digital health (e.g. electronic health data exchange) and actual use (e.g. high adoption of electronic health records) (Beckmann, et al., 2021). The experience of Estonia and Bahrain serves as a valuable reference for global digital health initiatives supported by the World Health Organisation (WHO), illustrating the feasibility and benefits of a transition to sophisticated health information systems (World Bank Group, 2015).

Digital health, often referred to as "health 4.0" or "connected health", represents a revolution in delivery, based on technological advances such as artificial intelligence, the Internet of Things (IoT), big data analysis and innovative IT systems. It encompasses all medical practices that integrate information and communication technologies (ICT) to improve prevention, diagnosis, treatment and healthcare management (Xavier, 2017). It includes a range of solutions from electronic medical records to telemedicine, promoting an integrated and efficient approach to health information management. It has the potential to revolutionise healthcare by giving patients more control over their health, empowering patients and transforming the doctor-patient relationship, thereby improving access to care (Topol, 2016).

Electronic medical records (EMRs) are seen as a key element in the digital transformation of the healthcare system. The implementation of an EMR promises various improvements, for example in terms of information availability, care coordination or patient safety, and is necessary for the analysis of megadata (Wurster, et al., 2024). This EMR is considered to be "an electronic record of an individual's healthcare information that is created, collected, managed and accessed by authorized clinicians and staff within a healthcare organization", and replaces internal clinical documentation on pre-printed paper charts (Wurster, et al., 2024).

Electronic medical records (EMRs) play a key role in improving the quality, safety and efficiency of healthcare. As they are increasingly implemented, computerised documentation produced directly by providers is tending to become the preferred means of producing narrative clinical documents (Patners in health, 2013). This documentation details the patient's history, current clinical situation and established care plan, providing an essential basis for medical follow-up and informed decision-making. All members of the clinical team refer to this documentation to share a common vision of the patient, while administrative departments exploit these stories to meet regulatory compliance requirements and justify healthcare benefits. It shapes the way healthcare services are described and justified, how medical decisions are recorded, and how clinicians communicate with each other. They promote shared decision-making, and are seen as a major means of delivering high-value care (Vos,

Boonstra, Kooistra, Seelen, & Offenbeek, 2020).

The transition to electronic medical records via healthcare information systems would improve the management of medical information, reduce the risk of medical errors and facilitate communication between the various players in the healthcare sector. This would help to improve the overall quality of care and enhance the continuity of treatment. This digital transformation of the healthcare system is seen as essential to meeting current and future societal challenges, such as the ageing of the population and rising healthcare costs, while maintaining a high quality of care and increasing digital maturity (Wurster, et al., 2024).

In line with these advances, the World Health Organisation (WHO) is actively encouraging the adoption of effective health information systems on a global scale, and is promoting a collaborative approach aimed at standardising practices and ensuring the interoperability of systems for effective health data management (World Health Organisation, 2013). Disease management is a major concern in the country. Health information systems would enable health data to be collected, analysed and shared rapidly, strengthening the ability to respond effectively to emergency situations. Real-time monitoring of epidemiological trends would facilitate a rapid and coordinated response to minimise the impact on public health.

Introducing and optimising health information systems in Haiti is a crucial step towards modernising the health sector and meeting the specific challenges facing the country. The interest of these undertakings revolves around multiple dimensions aimed at improving access to care, strengthening disease (or epidemic) management, optimising the use of limited resources, and adapting practices to cultural and social realities (PAHO, 2024). This adaptability is a key element. By taking into account local particularities and actively involving communities, health information systems can be shaped to meet Haiti's specific needs (PAHO, 2024). An approach that respects cultural norms acceptance of the system and promotes its effectiveness.

Collaboration between healthcare professionals from different disciplines is seen as a key factor in achieving high-quality patient care. The symptoms of many patients today, particularly those with chronic conditions, are complex and often require the collaboration of healthcare professionals from different medical specialties. To collaborate effectively, it is necessary to share knowledge and skills, integrate information and work as a cohesive healthcare team, often while in different locations (Vos, Boonstra, Kooistra, Seelen, & Offenbeek, 2020).

Thus, digital health and health information systems are introducing a new computer language into the medical field, aimed at optimising the effectiveness of care while guaranteeing the confidentiality and security of health data. This convergence between medicine and IT is creating an innovative landscape, redefining the delivery of healthcare in the age of digital connectivity (World Health Organization, 1997).

II. Haiti and digital health

At present, Haiti is a significant distance away from the era of digital health and transition to Health 4.0. The technological advances that characterise this new era, with their transformative potential for healthcare, remain a distant horizon for the country. A number of complex factors contribute to this reality, such as the absence of a fully operational health information system at national level. This results in a fragmentation of medical data, limiting the ability to have an overall view of the health of the population. The coordination of care between different regions of the country remains a challenge, hampering the provision of coherent and coordinated healthcare.

In paper archives, a traditional method of storing health prevailed, where physical files were used to record patients' medical data. These records were often filed manually, making data retrieval and analysis laborious and prone to error. In addition, this approach exposed the data to various risks, such as loss in the event of incidents such as floods or fires, and deterioration due to wear and tear on the paper. The lack of adequate follow-up was also a major problem, as it was difficult to trace patients' medical history and ensure continuity of care. This fragmentation of data often led to a loss of consistency in medical treatment and made coordination between healthcare professionals difficult, compromising the quality of overall healthcare (Medicai Record System, 2017). Thus, the paper-based health record management system in Haiti had many drawbacks and limited the effectiveness and efficiency of healthcare in the country.

Faced with these unique challenges in the healthcare sector, Haiti has seen the emergence of a variety of technological solutions, each bringing its own innovations and complexities. From their earliest beginnings to their current configuration, Haiti's HIS have undergone a series of transformations, adaptations and challenges. Despite the efforts of the government and certain international bodies, a number of challenges remain. The technologies used often have to be adapted to the specific needs of each healthcare establishment.

Some institutions have implemented HISs designed to manage electronic medical records at a local level, offering an individualised approach that simply covers their internal needs (PAHO, 2024). Although effective at institutional level, these systems can sometimes lack interoperability within the institution or with other institutions, creating challenges for information sharing between healthcare stakeholders. This diversity of coverage raises questions about the consistency of practices and standards at national level.

On the legal front, Article 323 of the Haitian Penal Code sets out the obligations of health professionals with regard to the confidentiality of medical data: "Doctors, surgeons and other health officers, as well as pharmacists, midwives and all other persons entrusted by their status or profession with secrets entrusted to them, who, except in cases where the law obliges them to act as whistleblowers, reveal these secrets, will be punished by imprisonment of between one month and one year" (Le Parlement Hai'tien, 1835). Although this article refers to the protection, security and confidentiality of medical information, it does so in a general and non-explicit manner. Indeed, the details of the specific measures to be adopted to guarantee this protection are not clearly defined.

Furthermore, there is currently no legislation in Haiti concerning the development of medical technologies, innovation and the implementation of new technologies in this field. Although these technologies can improve the information management procedures proposed by the Ministry of Public Health and Population, particularly data collection, there is no specific legal framework governing their adoption and use (PAHO, 2024).

Haiti, as a nation facing persistent socio-economic challenges, presents a complex landscape where health information systems interact with a myriad of economic, social and cultural variables (Providence, 2022). Firstly, the financial resources available to invest in healthcare infrastructure are limited, leading to challenges in implementing sophisticated technological solutions and achieving universal access to digital health services. In addition, economic inequalities exacerbated by poverty create disparities in access to health information systems, with vulnerable populations often having fewer opportunities to fully exploit these tools for their health (Medicai Record System, 2017).

Secondly, social, cultural and educational dynamics also influence how health information systems are perceived and used. Social norms around health, cultural beliefs and traditional care practices play an important role in the population's acceptance and adoption of health information systems. Thirdly, the physical and technological infrastructure available in Haiti also presents challenges for the development and use of HIS. Electricity , internet access problems and limited communications infrastructure can hamper the implementation of digital solutions (PAHO, 2024). In addition, availability of technical skills and qualified human resources to design, manage and SISs is a challenge in a context where resources are already limited.

During the surveys carried out, it was observed that institutions use a variety of applications at different workstations to record patients' medical data. Each workstation may use a separate application to manage specific aspects of care, such as exteme clinic, radiology, laboratory or billing, resulting in information being dispersed across several independent systems.

Despite the use of certain digital technologies, these institutions continue to practice the traditional method of collecting data on paper. Medical records, examination results and clinical notes are often first recorded manually before being transcribed onto a local or remote digital device. This hybrid process, while facilitating a certain form of digitisation, introduces redundancies and increases the risk of errors. The persistence of this dual method - manual and digital - poses challenges in terms of data consistency and integrity. Transcribing paper data onto digital media can be prone to input errors and omissions. In addition, the lack of integration between the different applications used at each workstation complicates the consolidation of medical information, thereby limiting effectiveness of care and the quality of patient management.

The data was collected from three (3) major institutions in the commune of Carrefour,

namely the Hòpital adventiste d'Haiti, the Centre
Hospitalier de Carrefour and Health and Wellness CLINIC, each with specific
practices related to the use of health information systems and varying levels of
adoption and implementation, making it possible to assess their effectiveness in
diverse contexts.

III. Fragmentation of health information systems at Carrefour

The methodology is directly inspired by the theory of imbrication (Providence, 2022),
examining each level independently while analysing their interactions. By focusing on
the integration of these systems in the delivery of healthcare, the aim is to examine
how digital technologies can improve the management of medical data, analyse their
effectiveness in processing large quantities of data, and thus contribute to a better
quality of care in this specific area while guaranteeing the integrity and confidentiality
of medical information.

Located around 10 km from Port-au-Prince, the Haitian capital, Carrefour is a rapidly
expanding urban area. However, this rapid growth is accompanied by major socio-
economic challenges that affect the ability of the local healthcare system to respond
effectively to the needs of the population. These contextual factors have a direct
impact on the management of healthcare and medical data. Demographically,
Carrefour is one of the most densely populated municipalities in the region
(Providence, 2022), which amplifies the challenges associated with managing
electronic medical records. Despite these challenges, Carrefour stands out for its
concentration of various healthcare institutions. This institutional diversity provides an
interesting basis for observing the dynamics of the healthcare sector in an expanding
urban environment.

The target population for this study is healthcare professionals directly involved in the
use of health information systems (HIS) to manage electronic medical records (EMR).
These players play a key role in the day-to-day running of healthcare services, and
their experience and expertise were essential in assessing the effectiveness and impact
of these systems on the quality of care. The participants include a wide range
professional profiles, including doctors, nurses and administrators or technicians
specialising in medical IT. This variety makes it possible to look at the use of SIS from
different angles, taking into account the specific features and needs of each
professional group in the context of managing electronic medical records.

The healthcare professionals who are the focus of this study work in a variety of
healthcare establishments, ranging from public and private hospitals to smaller
medical centres. These different types of establishments offer a comprehensive
perspective on the implementation and use of information systems in a variety of
healthcare contexts. These professionals have been selected on the basis of their active
role in the use of health information systems (HIS), which ensures that the responses
collected are directly linked to the actual experience of system users in their
professional practices.

In addition, selection of participants also took into account their knowledge of the clinical processes associated with the use of HIS in their respective institutions. This approach makes it possible to gather valuable information on the challenges encountered and the best practices adopted to improve the effectiveness of health information systems in managing electronic medical records.

In this context, it was essential to ensure that doctors, nurses and IT technicians, who each interact with health information systems in specific ways, were all adequately represented. In doing so, we increased the accuracy of the results obtained by taking into account the different professional perspectives on the use of health information systems, and ensured a comprehensive and nuanced view of the effectiveness of health information systems in the management of electronic medical records in the municipality of Carrefour.

During the surveys, two interview guides were designed to structure discussions with healthcare professionals involved in the use of health information systems (HIS). These guides were used to guide the discussions, while offering sufficient flexibility to allow in-depth exploration of each participant's experiences and perceptions. The aim was to understand how each professional, according to their role, perceives and interacts with these systems in the context of healthcare. By using well-defined interview guides, it was possible to gather valuable information on the various perspectives of these players, while encouraging a freer and more spontaneous approach on their part. This method made it possible to capture a variety of opinions and experiences, providing a rich and varied database reflecting the many facets of the use of HIS in the hospital environment.

During the course of the interviews, a number of recurring concepts emerged, highlighting the most crucial aspects of healthcare information systems. These included the challenges associated IT infrastructures, data security issues, the management of electronic medical records. These elements were studied in terms of their impact on the quality of healthcare. In addition to the technical and organisational aspects, participants also discussed the challenges encountered in the day-to-day use of the systems, including obstacles relating to training, resources and the adaptation of systems to local realities.

To ensure the quality of the data, all the interviews were transcribed. This facilitated a more in-depth analysis of the exchanges, allowing the researchers to revisit key elements and compare responses at different points in time. The transcripts were used to extract the most relevant points of view, while preserving the nuance of each utterance.

In context of this research, a sample of healthcare institutions was carefully selected to allow for diverse and representative data collection. Each institution, from large hospitals to smaller health centres, made an essential contribution to the evaluation of health information systems (HIS) in the commune of Carrefour. This diversity of institutions enabled a range of perspectives to be captured, fostering a more complete understanding of the health landscape in this region.

The aim of this selection was to ensure a qualitative approach, focusing on the experiences of healthcare professionals in different types of settings. Each institution provided detailed information about the implementation and use of electronic medical records (EMRs), and the unique challenges they face in adopting information systems. As such, this study aims to understand, beyond the numbers, the specific local realities and contexts.

The contrasting experiences observed in these institutions have provided a rich and nuanced picture of EMR management practices. Some facilities had advanced technological infrastructures, while others faced major limitations in terms of resources and equipment. These differences revealed significant variations in the adoption and use of SIS, while also highlighting common obstacles faced by these facilities.

This comparative analysis has been essential in capturing the nuances of health information management at Carrefour. By examining the way in which HIS is integrated and used within different institutions, the study has brought to light similarities and differences that shed light on current practices. For example, some institutions have adopted digital technologies more fluidly, while others have encountered resistance due to organisational or logistical challenges.

The choice of these institutions reflects the desire to take account of the variety of healthcare structures present in the municipality. By taking into account the size of the facilities, technological capabilities and access to digital resources, this study provides a balanced representation of the challenges encountered at different levels of the healthcare system. These contextual elements are essential for an in-depth understanding of the effectiveness of health information systems.

By analysing this diversity, the study also aims to highlight the factors that facilitate or hinder the adoption of EMRs, while taking into account the demographic, socio-economic and organisational differences of the institutions studied. The results obtained thus make it possible to compare the approaches and solutions implemented in different establishments, offering an insight into good practice and areas for improvement.

The qualitative method adopted enabled detailed data to be collected, not only on the technical infrastructure, but also on healthcare professionals' perceptions of the usefulness and effectiveness of HIS. This made it possible to capture personal accounts, opinions and suggestions that would not have emerged in a more general quantitative study.

This study offers an in-depth look the in which SISs influence management in Carrefour, while providing valuable insights for future initiatives to improve the healthcare system in Haiti. Combining the different experiences and data collected in these establishments enables a comparative analysis to be drawn up, while contributing to the formulation of practical recommendations adapted to local realities.

Graph 1. Comparison of the use of the manual and digital systems at
Carrefour

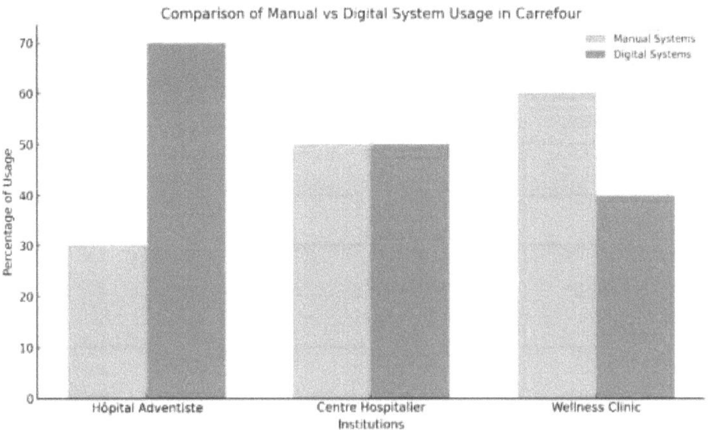

Sources: Authors' survey in 2024

This graph compares the use of manual and digital systems in three healthcare
institutions in Carrefour, and illustrates the fragmentation of systems and the persistent
reliance on traditional methods.

Graph 2. Challenges identified in the SIS at Carrefour

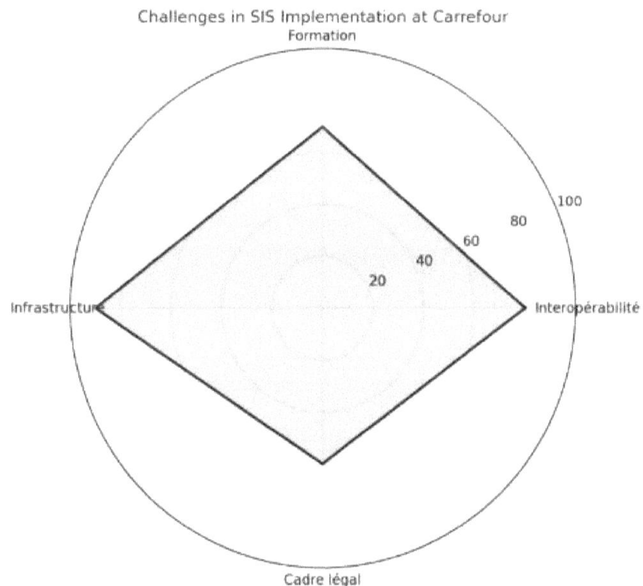

Sources: Authors' survey in 2024

This radar chart highlights the main challenges in setting up SISs (interoperability, training, infrastructure, legal framework) and their relative seriousness.

1. *Interoperability*

The systems used in different institutions cannot exchange data seamlessly. There is a lack of common standards for data formats. Possible solutions would be :

- standards such as FHIR (Fast Healthcare Interoperability Resources) to standardise data formats;
- Create a centralised infrastructure where all establishments share data;
- Training technical staff in interoperability standards to integrate existing systems.

2. *Staff training*

The lack of skills among hospital staff in using and managing HIS is a serious challenge. In addition, the implementation of a viable solution must take into account resistance to technological change among stakeholders. Possible solutions include

- Organise regular workshops on the use of digital tools (Microsoft Access, FileMaker, etc.);
- Educate staff about the benefits of SIS in reducing resistance;
- Involve international or regional experts to supervise local staff.

3. *Infrastructure*

The lack of digital devices (computers, servers), limited Internet connections and frequent power cuts do not make it easy to set up the SIS. In this case, the possible solutions would be :

- Modernise the equipment with with terminals for each workstation

and secure servers;

- Install energy solutions such as solar panels to compensate for power cuts;
- Combine local and remote storage to guarantee access to data in the event of failure.

4. *Legal framework*

The absence of specific laws to protect medical data and regulate the use technologies is a major obstacle. Possible solutions would be :

- Develop legislation to guarantee the confidentiality, integrity and security of medical data;
- Incorporate clear rules to protect SIS against cyber attacks;
- Introduce guidelines to encourage the development and adoption of health technologies.

5. *Access to and use of data*

The difficulty doctors and patients have in accessing records in real time poses a serious problem in terms of quality of care. This is because the data is often incomplete or poorly consolidated, making it impossible to provide intelligent patient care. In this case, the possible solutions would be :

- Develop a simple user interface to access medical data in real time;
- Connect all services (laboratory, radiology, clinic) on a single platform;
- Mehre in rnuvre systems with synchronisation in time

synchronization for
avoid redundancy.

These recommendations, combined with a strong institutional commitment, can transform the use of HIS in Carrefour, improving the quality of care and the management of medical data. The lack of technical standardisation limits interaction with other levels, particularly social (user skills) and organisational (lack of common policy). These social factors amplify the technical limitations, exacerbating data errors and delays in care. Organisational challenges also weaken technical and social efforts, creating an environment where digital initiatives struggle thrive.

HISs play a central role in global digital health, efficient management of medical data. However, their adoption in Carrefour is hampered by socio-economic, technological and cultural factors.

The effectiveness of SIS at Carrefour is limited by structural and technological shortcomings. However, by applying the proposed solutions, it is possible to significantly improve EMR management and the quality of care. The lessons learned from international cases can serve as a guide for a transformation adapted to the Haitian context.

IV.   Qualitative analyses developed by SIS at Carrefour

In order to develop the qualitative analyses for this study, I will be taking a closer look at the observations and perceptions gathered from the players involved (healthcare professionals, administrators and technicians) in Carrefour's healthcare institutions. These analyses will focus on the technical, social and organisational dimensions according to the interweaving theory.

Figure 3: Circular diagram showing the distribution of impacts between medical errors and delays

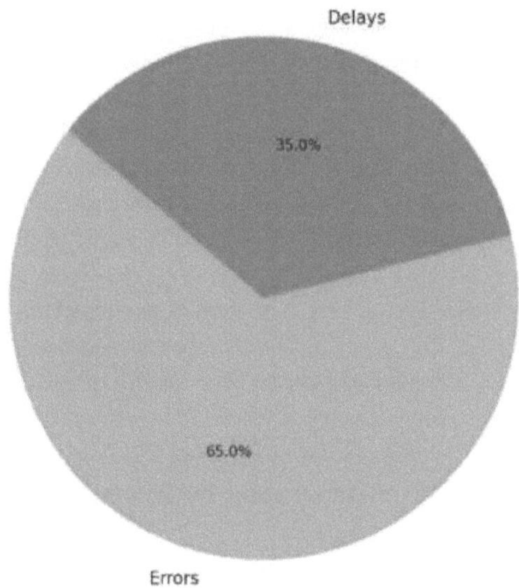

Sources: Authors' survey in 2024

1. *Technical level: Systems fragmentation*

Institutions use a combination systems (Microsoft Excel, Otus CMS, FileMaker) that do not communicate with each other. In 60% of cases, medical data is initially collected on paper before being transcribed, increasing the risk of errors. Frequent power cuts limit access to digital tools, hampering continuity of care.

Technological fragmentation hinders the fluidity of information flows, creating data silos within each institution. Users complain about the slowness of the tools, particularly when searching medical data in unconsolidated paper or digital archives. Poorly consolidated data makes epidemiological analysis and strategic planning at local level difficult. This explains how technological shortcomings amplify users' frustrations, limiting their adoption of HIS.

2. *Social level: User skills and attitudes*

Only 30% of users surveyed have received specific training on the digital tools used. A significant proportion of staff prefer paper-based systems, arguing that they are faster and more reliable in a context of frequent breakdowns. Double data entry (paper and digital) adds to the administrative burden, creating additional stress.

Users' reluctance to adopt digital systems is exacerbated by a lack of training and technical support. The perception that digital tools increase the workload reflects a mistrust of their effectiveness and reliability. These attitudes underline the need for ongoing support, not only technical but also psychological, to reduce resistance to change. User attitudes are also influenced by the lack of clear guidelines and institutional support.

3. Organisational level: Legal framework and processes

Each institution develops its own data management protocols, with no national coordination. There are no clear guidelines for healthcare professionals on the management and protection of medical data. Insufficient budgets prevent the acquisition and maintenance of modern technologies.

The lack of a regulatory framework reinforces organisational fragmentation, with non-standardised processes between institutions (Providence, 2022). Administrative managers recognise that the lack of funding is a major obstacle to the adoption of digital technologies. Without a shared strategic vision at local and national level, the individual efforts of institutions are ineffective in solving global challenges. The lack of a centralised infrastructure is a clear example of how institutions are unable to work together coherently.

These in-depth qualitative analyses enrich this research by highlighting the perceptions and human interactions that influence the effectiveness of HIS in Carrefour. In order to improve the Health Information Systems (HIS) in the municipality of Carrefour, here is an analysis of the existing tools and the improvements needed at each level, based on the observations and results of the study. With these improvements, Carrefour's HIS can become a model for medical data management in similar contexts, optimising the quality of care and the efficiency of processes.

V. Possible digital solutions

To resolve the challenges identified and improve the Health Information Systems (HIS) at Carrefour, here are some concrete examples of technological tools that can be adapted to the local context. These tools are selected on the basis of their ability to meet the specific needs of HIS while being accessible and compatible with low-resource environments (Medicai Record System, 2017; Patners in health, 2013).

1. Integrated platform for managing electronic medical records (EMR)

OpenMRS (Open Medicai Record System)

Why choose it :

- Onen source system, designed for low-resource environments;
- Allows customisation to suit local needs;
- Offers robust functionality for EMR management, interoperability and data analysis.

Advantages :

- Free, with a large community of supporters;
- Possible integration with public health tools such as DHIS2.

How to use :

- Pent centralises the medical data of Carrefour institutions.

DHIS2 (District Health Information Software 2)

Why choose it :
- System for managing skipped data widely used in developing countries;
- Ideal for large-scale data monitoring and management.

Advantages :
- Real-time data visualization via dashboards;
- Compatible with tools such as OpenMRS for an integrated system.

How to use :
- Monitoring key health indicators (mortality, vaccination, etc.) for Carrefour.

2. *Standards and Interoperability*

FHIR (Fast Healthcare Interoperability Resources)

Why choose it :
- International standard for health data exchange ;
- Facilitates interoperability between different tools and systems.

Advantages :
- Flexible and compatible with systems such as OpenMRS and DHIS2 ;
- Suitable for contexts requiring communication between several institutions.

How to use :
- Integrate FHIR as standard for exchanging of data between the

institutions.

3. *Safeguarding and Accessibility*

Google Workspace for Healthcare

Why choose it :
- Affordable cloud platform for storing medical data;
- Secure and compliant with international standards such as HIPAA.

Advantages :
- Provides real-time access to data;
- Easier collaboration between healthcare professionals via Google Docs, Sheets,

etc.

How to use :
- Use Google Drive to back up data from local institutions.

AWS HealthLake

Why choose it :
- Cloud solution specially designed to manage healthcare data;
- Compatible with FHIR standards.

Advantages :
- High reliability and safety ;
- Advanced data analysis using artificial intelligence.

How to use :
- To centralise and analyse health data at Carrefour.

4. *User interfaces and mobile applications*

CommCare

Why choose it :
- Open source mobile application for collecting and managing health data;
- Designed for low-resource environments.

Advantages :
- Works in non-league mode, with automatic data synchronisation;
- Used for case management and data collection in the field.

How to use :
- For Carrefour's community hopping agents, lem enabling data to be collected in real time.

M'Hero

Why choose it :
- Two-way communication tool between health authorities and healthcare workers;
- you to share alerts in real time and gather feedback.

Advantages :
- Works on basic phones via SMS;
- Can be integrated with DHIS2.

How to use :
- To send notifications and coordinate activities between healthcare establishments.

5. *Data Visualisation and Analysis*

Table

Why choose it :
- Powerful data visualization tool ;
- Allows to create tables of dashboards dashboards toanalyse the SIS performance.

Advantages :
- Easy to use with data from a variety of sources;
- Compatible with databases such as OpenMRS.

How to use :
- To analyse trends in medical data at Carrefour.

Power BI

Why choose it :
- Microsoft tool for data analysis ;
- Ideal generating automated reports.

Advantages :
- Easy integration with Excel, often used in local institutions.

How to use :
- To improve the production of reports from existing management systems.

6. *Training and awareness-raising*

LearnDash

Why choose it :
- E-learning platform that can be customised for specific needs.

Advantages :

- Enables users' progress to be monitored and their learning to be assessed.

How to use :

- Training medical staff in the use of new digital tools.

OpenWHO

Why choose it :

- Free training platform offered by the WHO.

Advantages :

- Courses adapted to various contexts, y including digital health.

How to use :

- Raising awareness of best practice in digital health among Carrefour healthcare professionals.

These tools can be introduced gradually to maximise adoption and minimise initial costs. Their effectiveness will also depend on strategic integration and ongoing institutional support. For example, OpenMRS, an open-sourced electronic medical record (EMR) system, offers a number of significant advantages for the health sector in Haiti, particularly in the commune of Carrefour.

Conclusion

The effectiveness of SIS at Carrefour depends on better integration of the technical, social and organisational dimensions. Drawing on the theory of interweaving, this study proposes an integrative approach to overcoming the challenges identified. Inspired by international success stories, these recommendations can guide the transformation of SISs in Haiti towards better management of EMR and improved care.

The theory of imbrication reveals that the failures of the SIS at Carrefour cannot be tackled in isolation. For example:

- The adoption of a high-performance technical system (such as FHIR) requires solid organisational policies and appropriate training;
- The   gaps   social, such   such as   resistance   to   change,
    limit

the effectiveness of technical investments.

The analysis carried out as part of this study highlights the strategic importance of health information systems (HIS) in managing electronic medical records, and in improving the quality and continuity of care. These digital tools play a central role in the collection, management and interpretation of medical data, while at the same time promoting informed decision-making by healthcare professionals. Nevertheless, in the context of the Carrefour municipality, the implementation of HIS is hampered by structural, technological and human challenges, limiting their potential to transform healthcare in the long term.

The lack of interoperability between establishments, inconsistencies in the data collected and the inadequacy of digital management policies were identified as major obstacles. These weaknesses compromise not only the fluidity of information exchanges, but also coordination between the various players involved in the care pathway. In addition, there are issues relating to the security and protection of patients' medical data.

To meet the challenges raised, it is essential to strengthen technological infrastructures and promote clear policies on digital governance. Emphasis should be placed on training healthcare professionals, establishing robust interoperability mechanisms through common standards such as FHIR, and developing appropriate regulatory frameworks. These initiatives could transform SISs into real levers for progress, contributing to better integration of care, fewer medical errors and more personalised care for patients.

This research lays the groundwork for further reflection on the transition to sustainable and equitable digital health. The results call for further research, particularly into the mechanisms of adoption and use of HIS in similar contexts. This work could inspire global strategies aimed at strengthening healthcare systems in Haiti, while integrating the socio-cultural and technological dimensions specific to each context.

Bibliography

1. World Bank, G. (2024, November 6). The World Bank in Haiti. Retrieved December 9, 2024, from World Bank Group: https://www.banquemondiale.org/fr/country/haiti/overview

2. Beckmann, M., Dittmer, K., Jaschke, J., Karbach, U., Köberlein-Neu, J., & Nocon, M. (2021). Electronic patient record and its effects on social aspects of interprofessional collaboration and clinical workflows in hospitals (eCoCo): a mixed methods study protocol. BMC Health Services Research. doi:10.1186/s12913-021-06377-5

3. Embi, P. J., Weir, C., Efthimiadis, E. N., Thielke, S. M., Hedeen, A. N., & Hammond, K. W. (2013). Computerized provider documentation: findings and implications of a multisite study of clinicians and administrators. doi:10.1136/amiajnl-2012-000946

4. World Bank Group. (2015, February 02). Health sector reform : Bahrain follows Estonia's lead. Retrieved from https://www.banquemondiale.org/fr/news/feature/2015/02/02/lessons-from-estoniahow-bahrain-is-looking-to-improve-its-healthcare

5. The Haitian Parliament. (1835). Penal Code of the Republic of Haiti. Port-au-Prince: Le Moniteur.

6. Medicai Record System (2017, April 17). Partners in Health Haiti EMR. Retrieved November 29, 2020, from OpenMRS.

7. World Health Organisation. (1997). Health informatics and telemedicine - EB99/30. World Health Organisation.

8. World Health Organization. (2013). Resolution on eHealth standardization and interoperability - WHA66.24. Brussels: World Health Organization.

9. World Health Organization. (2021). Global Digital Health Strategy 2020-2025. World Health Organization.

10. PAHO. (2024, September 22). Haiti Country Profile. Retrieved June 11, 2024,

from Pan American Health Organization:
https://hia.paho.org/en/countries-22/haiti-country-profile

H.Patners in health (2013, July 13). Open-source EMR: A New Model for Evidence-based Health Care in Haiti. Retrieved November 21, 2024, from Patners in health.

12. Providence, C. (2022). The Paradoxes of Change in Haiti: Public Policies and Territorial Development. Pointe-à-Pitre: Presses Universitaires des Antilles.

13. Topol, E. (2016). The Patient Will See You Now: The Future of Medicine Is in Your Hands. New York: Basic Books; Illustrated edition.

14. Vos, J. F., Boonstra, A., Kooistra, A., Seelen, M., & Offenbeek, M. v. (2020). The influence of electronic health record use on collaboration among medical specialties. BMC Health Serv Res. doi: https://doi.org/10.1186/s12913-020-05542-6

15. Wurster, F., Beckmann, M., Cecon-Stabel, N., Dittmer, K., Hansen, T. J., Jaschke, J., . . Karbach, U. (2024). The Implementation of an Electronic Medical Record in a German Hospital and the Change in Completeness of Documentation. Longitudinal Document Analysis.

16. Xavier, C. (2017). Santé 4.0. Paris: Georg Éditeur.

Part II

Digital transformation and education

Setting the context for Part Two

Digital Transformation and Education

Education is one of the areas where digital transformation could have the most profound impact, not only by modernising teaching practices, but also by reducing inequalities in access to learning. In Haiti, where systemic challenges such as inadequate educational infrastructure, poor teacher training and geographical disparities limit access to quality education, information and communication technologies (ICTs) are emerging as an essential lever for transforming the sector. However, this digital transition is taking place in a context marked by a digital divide that reflects and exacerbates existing socio-economic inequalities.

Context and issues

The role of ICT in higher education is increasingly recognised as a necessary condition for improving the quality of education and preparing learners for the demands of a globalised, digital society. However, in Haiti, the integration of ICT into educational establishments remains uneven. Faced with limited Internet access, inadequate equipment and a lack of training in digital skills, students and teachers are struggling to exploit the full potential of technological tools.

The digital divide in Haiti goes beyond infrastructure. It includes gaps in skills, in the ability to use technologies pedagogically and in access to digital resources. These inequalities have a direct impact on students' academic performance and teachers' ability to modernise their practices. As a result, education in Haiti is at a crucial juncture, where strategic adoption of ICT can reduce barriers to learning while expanding opportunities for marginalised populations.

Objectives of the game

This second part of the book explores the impact of ICTs on education in Haiti, focusing on disparities access, teachers' perceptions and practices, and strategies for sustainable educational transformation. Its chapters analyse :

1. The impact of the digital divide on students' academic performance, highlighting how inequalities in digital access translate into gaps in academic results;

2. The perceptions and practices of university teachers with regard to the integration of ICT, identifying opportunities and obstacles to the adoption of these technologies;

3. Avenues for sustainable digital transformation, highlighting solutions for strengthening digital infrastructures, skills and management in educational establishments.

Approach and articulation

The analyses presented in this section are based on a combination of quantitative and qualitative methods, including field surveys and case studies. They draw on both social theories, such as Pierre Bourdieu's theory of educational inequality, and models of the pedagogical integration of ICT. This dual approach provides a nuanced understanding of the dynamics at play and enables us to formulate concrete recommendations tailored to the Haitian context.

In exploring these issues, this section reveals that ICTs can play a key role in modernising education in Haiti, but only if strategic steps are taken to bridge the digital divide and support teachers and students. It also emphasises that digital transformation in higher education requires a collaborative approach between government, educational institutions and international partners to ensure an inclusive and sustainable transition.

ICT in higher education: Impact of the digital divide on academic performance
Ms Rachelle CHARLES
Research assistant at the CRS-IUS in Haiti.
Dr Jean Rony GUSTAVE
Associate researcher, CRS-IUS d'Haiti.

Introduction

Today's educational environment has specific characteristics that make students face up to their responsibilities in the learning process. The gradual integration of digital technology into education has led educational players to adapt in order to respond to this new context and to the new challenges that have revolutionised access to knowledge and the associated pedagogy. This so-called digital transformation is "changing the traditional organisation of teaching and learning situations. The use of computerised products certainly leads to a break with the units of time, action and place of traditional training" (Blamont 99). The question of the mechanisms for integrating technology into higher education has also been raised.

In Haiti, for example, "information and communication technologies have been strongly promoted in the education sector, particularly through the efforts of the Université d'État d'Haiti (UEH) and numerous national and international public and private bodies [...]" (Jean-Jacques and Oxiné 344). The adoption of technological tools in education is nonetheless prompting reflection on the pedagogy of teaching in a digital context and the transformation that this implies. This transition is accompanied by difficulties in effectively integrating ICT into the education system, particularly in vulnerable contexts where access to technological tools remains limited.

Whether in terms of teaching practices, pedagogy or educational governance, educational institutions adapting and positioning themselves in relation to digital technology. Depending on their skills, available resources and prospects for incorporating digital technology, some institutions have a higher level integration than others. This heterogeneity in the integration and use of digital technology creates a divide that affects all stakeholders, particularly students, in terms the effective use of tools, the development of digital skills and, ultimately, their academic results.

The objectives of this work are to assess the integration of digital technology into teaching practices, by analysing governance, digital pedagogy, and the impacts and challenges of digital transformation. It also explores the links between digital disparities and academic success in these higher education institutions (HEIs).

The following hypotheses were formulated: (1) the use of technological tools in HEIs enhances students' skills in the acquisition of academic knowledge; and (2) those benefiting from adequate training in digital skills are more likely to succeed academically in a context of digital transformation.

To carry out this work, a dual qualitative and quantitative approach was used, providing a more complete and nuanced understanding of the phenomena studied, with aim of grasping the complexity of the behaviour of the players involved. On the one hand, the qualitative dimension includes an inventory of current teaching practices, an assessment of available resources, an exploration of the level digital integration and an analysis of how the digital divide manifests itself from one student to another. The analysis also takes account of specific social determinants, thus providing a detailed overview of the context of digital integration. On the other hand, the quantitative dimension of the research focused on assessing academic success in relation to the level of access to technology, through the use of a survey questionnaire.

Stratified probability sampling was used to select higher education institutions (HEIs), distinguishing between public (UEH) and private institutions, while respecting inclusion criteria, including digital integration at different levels. Non-probability sampling was used to select the target population, including administrative/teaching staff, students, etc.

The data were collected from 23 July to 20 August 2024 in four (4) HEIs in the commune of Jacmel, the geographical area of the study. Jacmel is located in the south-east of Haiti and is the capital of the country. According to figures from the Institut Hai'tien de Statistique et d'Informatique (IHSI), the population was 187,253 in 2015 (A.-L. Kem).

Jacmel's education system is made up of both public and private establishments. In terms of higher and vocational education, the city has a number of specialised institutions, including around ten IESs (public, private, UEH). In the 1980s, most of the city's young schoolchildren had to go to Port-au-Prince or leave the country, often for the Dominican Republic, to continue with their higher education, even though there were already some services on offer in the city.

However, in recent years, the number of university courses on offer in Jacmel has increased considerably, in response to growing demand and the difficulties of mobility to the country's capital. Despite this increase in provision, there are still limitations, particularly with regard to the integration of digital technology into higher education, which justifies the choice of Jacmel as the study area for this research.

I. Understanding the digital divide through the prism of Pierre Bourdieu and Connectivism

Pierre Bourdieu's social theories of education highlight the social nature of education, showing how education changes with society (René). First of all, he highlights the cultural arbitrariness of educational action, which favours certain social and linguistic norms and codes, which in turn enhance the cultural capital held by the dominant classes. The dominant classes find it easier to acquire and mobilise the cultural capital valued by the educational institution, which reinforces their position of power and social privilege. This theory is all the more interesting in the light of Christophe Michaut's success factors, in particular the way in which students study (whether or not they use digital technology), the context which they study (pedagogy) and their living conditions (financial resources) all have an impact on their academic progress and performance (Michaut).

On the assumption that the digital divide will have repercussions on a student's academic performance, the relative y disparities will thus contribute to exacerbating the inequalities that are perpetuated in the context of university institutions, given the differences in digital integration.

Technological advances and the way they are incorporated into university teaching methods mean that students have to develop and use skills to adapt. In his 1959 article *The School class as a social system*, cited by (Khôi), Parsons shows how, in a technologically advanced society such as that of the United States, the school has become the main agent of socialisation and selection. It internalises in pupils the general values of society, the skills and attitudes that are essential preconditions for fulfilling their future roles. Technological advances and their integration into university teaching methods mean that students have to develop and mobilise the skills they need to adapt.

And depending on their level of adaptation, likened by Parsons to a selection agent, students will or will not reach a certain academic level. Indeed, they highlight differences in the chances of success for learners from different socio-economic backgrounds. If these social inequalities are not addressed, they risk constituting a barrier to the integration and effective use of digital tools, which are essential for an inclusive education that is adapted to contemporary challenges.

Whereas Bourdieu's social theories of education highlight social inequalities as an obstacle to equitable access to education, and therefore to Information and Communication Technologies for Education (ICT4E), particularly through economic, cultural and social capital, connectivism emphasises the growing importance of digital technology as a lever for learning in an interconnected world. Connectivism is a theory of learning that emphasises the role of social networks and mobile technologies in facilitating learning. Stephen Downes quoted by (Jean Evulu).

This approach, proposed by George Siemens and Stephen Downes in the early 2000s, argues that learning is not limited to one person or to a traditional learning environment, but is seen as a distributed process in which individuals interact with their environment and with others.

As Siemens points out in the digital age, connectivism represents learning model that takes account of the tectonic transformations in society, where learning is no longer an individualistic internal activity (Bates). From this perspective, connections between individuals, ideas, resources and concepts are seen as essential for learning. It also highlights the fact that learning is not limited to human interaction, but can also involve non-human devices.

II. ICT in higher education: between integration, transformation and digital transition

Whether in Haiti, Canada, France or the United States, the integration of new technologies in education, particularly in higher education, and the challenges posed by digital technology are not a matter for indifference and certainly cannot be left to chance. The players involved need to be made aware the issues and the impact of digital technology, as well as the strategies and political will required for effective integration. This means integrating digital tools such as computers, tablets, educational software, online applications, virtual learning and other technological devices into the teaching and learning process.

The impact of technology on education is a complex and much debated subject. On the one hand, proponents argue that integration of technology can improve the effectiveness of learning, while on the other hand critics point to concerns such as over-dependence on technology, inequalities of access to technological resources, and sometimes the potential distraction effect. Some authors, such as Stéphanie Roussel and Levy Pierre, stress that teaching should take over from technology, while others, such as Mangenot François, Bernard Cornu and Jean-Pierre Véran, argue that we need to go beyond the use of technology within educational establishments and accompany digital technology with a pedagogical project.

Mangenot François, Eddie Playfair and Jeong Kim, for their part, argue that y there are many challenges relating to this transformation, and that in this case it is important to put pedagogy at the centre and let it be enriched by technology. So a sustainable transition towards integration of digital tools in higher education means finding a balance with traditional teaching methods. This requires a strategic and considered approach, where technologies are integrated in a way that effectively supports educational objectives.

And while the integration of digital technology into education is an important first step, it paves the way for a more profound transformation, in which technology becomes a lever for change at the service of education. Digital transformation is a complex concept that encompasses a variety of aspects and cannot be reduced to a homogenous or one-dimensional definition.

It represents a set of major changes in educational practices and even in the way in which learning and teaching are envisaged. In the context of this work, the following definition will be considered:

Digital transformation in education is the application of digital technology and Internet information systems to the field of education to improve the quality of teaching, learning and educational management. This includes improving teaching methods, improving equipment and learning materials, and improving the experience of pupils, students and training participants (Kazimierz 5).

Digital transformation offers unprecedented opportunities in the way education is conceived and in the preparation of learners to succeed in an increasingly digitised society. This technological revolution offers new opportunities and also raises significant challenges. Indeed, digital activities have beneficial effects on learning. Digital platforms have become indispensable in managing the teaching and learning process. For some years now in Haiti, computer courses have been compulsory from secondary school level, and are a concrete example of this evolution, ensuring that students acquire the digital skills essential to succeed in the modern world.

It should also be stressed that digital transformation prepares students to meet the demands of today's job market, where mastery of technology has become indispensable in many professional fields. However, in some cases they could be detrimental, such as when students get distracted by social networks or plagiarise documents in league.

This digital transformation and its impact on education in higher education institutions are therefore not without ambiguity. Some institutions are embarking on the process of digital integration without giving sufficient consideration to digital pedagogy and management, which could compromise the effectiveness of their initiatives. Assessing the real impact of the use of digital tools on academic performance would involve taking a census of their use by students, while taking into account their academic performance and teaching contexts. It is essential to take account of the various challenges and issues associated with digital transformation, otherwise it being compromised and deepening existing divides.

Universities are changing. "The computerisation of universities began in the early 1980s and Internet use became widespread in the mid-1990s". (Ben Youssef and Rallet 11). They are developing strategies to become autonomous and to integrate into globalisation. The involvement of multilateral organisations, such as the United Nations Educational, Scientific and Cultural Organisation (UNESCO), the World Bank, the Organisation for Economic Co-operation and Development (OECD), etc., in formulating the international university agenda is shifting the boundaries of higher education beyond national societies. As with globalisation, digital technologies are increasingly at the heart of these strategies, gaining in importance in teaching practices.

All these transformations are not without impact. Technologies offer a prospect of pedagogical renewal and modernisation of higher education establishments. The current digital practices of students and teachers potentially influence academic performance, because of the added value of technologies in teaching and learning. Some empirical research indicates that potential of technology encourages the emergence of new learning styles. In fact, according to the report by the Canadian Council on Learning (CCL), "access to learning technologies in schools opens up a vast horizon of possibilities and contributes to the effectiveness of learning and teaching. The use of computers and the Internet for educational purposes expands learning opportunities for students and is a valuable teaching resource for teachers" (Jean Loisier 59).

The challenges are no less significant. They include the need for technological infrastructure, inequalities of access, the lack of technological skills among teachers, resistance to change, keeping students engaged and motivated online, and adapting traditional pedagogies to digital environments. The problematic nature of the relationship between pedagogy and technology can be seen in the gap that often exists between ideals and the reality of practice.

A sustainable transition to integration of digital technologies in higher education involves finding a balance with traditional teaching methods. This requires a strategic and considered approach, where technologies are integrated in a way that effectively supports educational objectives. Digital technology does indeed have a major role to play in education, particularly higher education, where the variety of uses ranges from enriching educational content to globalising training.

Technological tools make it possible to stimulate exchanges between the various players (learners, teachers), to encourage learners to become more involved in the learning process, and to provide better access to educational resources. They also make it possible to go beyond the physical setting by opening up university education to groups hitherto excluded because of their timetables and other commitments. This is the case, for example, for adults with busy working or family lives, people with reduced mobility who do not wish to or cannot necessarily travel to the learning , etc.

The use of ICT goes further than the pedagogical aspect or even easier access to training. In fact, apart from providing access to a distance learning room, ICTs, when used wisely, encourage collaboration and teamwork and, thanks to the digital skills that will be developed by using them, will also prepare users in some way for the job market.

The use of ICTE also affects the management of HEIs. Some tools and software make it easier to manage processes that used to take a lot of time, such as the registration process, online payments and the management of student databases (grades, courses taken, etc.).

All these changes are having an impact not only on teaching methods in HEIs, but also on different perceptions of teaching. More and more HEIs are offering distance learning courses, students and researchers are mobile, campuses are becoming 'digital' and teaching is globalised, making it an open and competitive space.

The configuration of higher education in contemporary societies is acquiring an increasingly relational dimension, i.e. universities and their respective countries are constantly comparing themselves on the basis of indicators expressing the national and international prestige of each of them. There is every reason to believe that the emergence of world rankings has transformed higher education into an open arena for competition, whether overt or latent, with a view to acquiring academic and social prestige that will be exploited to attract financial resources for the institutions ranked. (Martins 4)

The integration of ICT into education must go beyond its use to focus on measurable improvements in teaching and learning outcomes. While these tools have the potential to improve education, they can also be used in counterproductive ways. The role of ICT in student success is not universally accepted by researchers or authors writing on the subject.

Some authors believe that they play an indirect role insofar as ICT impacts the educational environment and access to educational resources. Others, such as Leuven E. et al, Terry N., Lewer J. J. & Macy A., believe that they have no impact on students' academic results; on the contrary, Kulik J. A. states that students who used ICT-based teaching obtained better results than those who did not use computers (Ben Youssef and Dahmani). (Ben Youssef and Dahmani).

III. The digital divide and academic performance

The inequalities associated with the digital divide are manifold. While the challenges of access are frequently cited, the lack of digital skills and the uses to which they are put can also exacerbate these disparities. They (Brotcome and Valenduc) explain that although "traditionally focused on the inequalities associated with physical access to ICTs, attention has gradually shifted to the social inequalities associated with their use, once the barrier of access is overcome". It should be noted, however, that social or economic inequalities can also have an impact on the level of access.

In economic terms, the cost of Internet equipment and services is a major obstacle for many people. In terms of accessibility, the availability of quality internet services is often uneven, especially in rural or less developed regions. In addition, the availability of technological tools on the local market also varies, affecting access for potential users.

In fact, income is the factor with the greatest impact on Internet access. Economically vulnerable people with limited access to digital technologies are the most likely to be affected by digital disparities. On a social level, authors such as Jan Van Dijk are interested in the process leading to the acquisition of digital skills and the factors that influence them (Van Dijk). According to Glassey O. and Pfister-Giauque B., some studies show that there is a real dialectic between the "digital culture" of individuals, on the one hand, and their "social inclusion" on the other, which gives them more or less opportunity to develop these skills (Brotcome and Valenduc).

Hargittaü E. demonstrates "the importance of social support in acquiring the skills needed to take full advantage of the benefits offered by online tools" (Brotcome and Valenduc). He also points out that "the fact of being on the margins of social circuits, both educational and professional, proves to be a considerable factor in digital exclusion" (Brotcome and Valenduc). From an institutional point of view, digital disparities can also be explained by a lack of support and investment from the State. The delay in implementing digital transformation policies within HEIs in Haiti is notable.

The lack of clear strategies and adequate funding for digital training and infrastructure prevents these institutions from bridging the digital divide and ensuring equitable access to technology for all students and staff. Digital disparities are therefore the result of a complex combination of economic, cultural, personal and institutional factors, each of which requires specific attention if it is to be addressed effectively. In addition, a lack of regulatory frameworks, the absence of public-private partnerships, the lack of support for innovation and digital entrepreneurship, and the absence of programmes to develop digital skills all reinforce the digital divide within the population.

As the research is both qualitative and quantitative, the research methods, tools and strategies have been clearly defined. This approach made it possible to analyse the manifestation of the digital divide from one student to another, taking into account specific social determinants and challenges relating to the digital infrastructure of

HEIs, thus providing a detailed overview of the context of digital integration. To establish our sampling frame, we mapped the HEIs in Jacmel, delimiting the city and referring to the list of recognised HEIs published on the website of the Ministry of National Education and Vocational Training. With exception of IUS, which is legally recognised, but

not present on the site due to an updating problem. Based on this mapping, an initial list of schools that have already begun to integrate technology into their teaching practices and operations has been drawn up.

Once the HEIs had been selected, quantitative data was collected from a total of 120 students in the four HEIs. Participants were anonymised using codes in order to preserve the confidentiality of the information shared as part of this study. The main objective of our choice of sample was to select a small number of individuals representative of the student population of the target institutions. For the other data collection methods, such as interviews, observations and individual interviews, we used non-probability sampling procedures.

Participants are students (currently enrolled in the HEIs selected for the survey), administrative staff, and teachers from these institutions. To ensure a diverse perspective, we have included both public and private universities, of different sizes and offering different levels integration of digital technologies into their programmes. By focusing on institutions that are already integrating or beginning to integrate technologies, we can better assess the effects and challenges of this integration. It also allows us to select a representative sample of current practices in Jacmel, providing more accurate and meaningful results.

The data collected indicates that the majority of students (50%) do not have access to any support or assistance from the HEIs they attend. In the context of learning in the digital age, where the use of technological tools has become essential, these unassisted students may encounter additional difficulties in accessing information, taking part in online courses and completing their academic work, thereby jeopardising their academic results.

Figure 1. Support provided by the HEIs

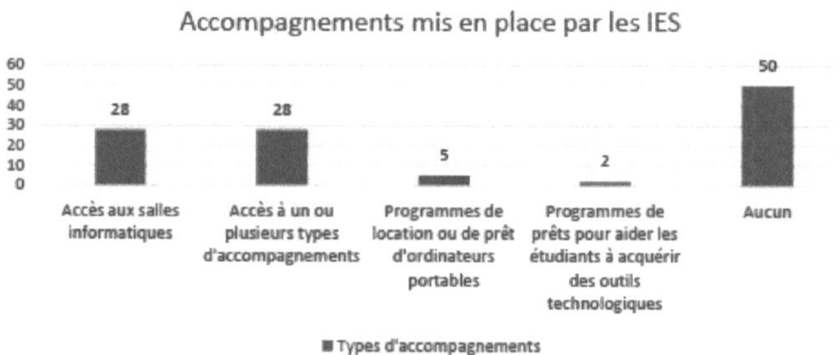

Figure 1 Support provided by HEIs Sources: Data collected by the authors

Around 28% of students benefit one or more types of support, including a laptop hire or loan scheme (5%) at one of the target HEIs, a loan scheme to acquire the technological tools they need for their studies (2%), a technical support service for installing, configuring and solving problems with technological tools, etc. 28% of them have access to a computer room.

Figure 2: Students' digital skills

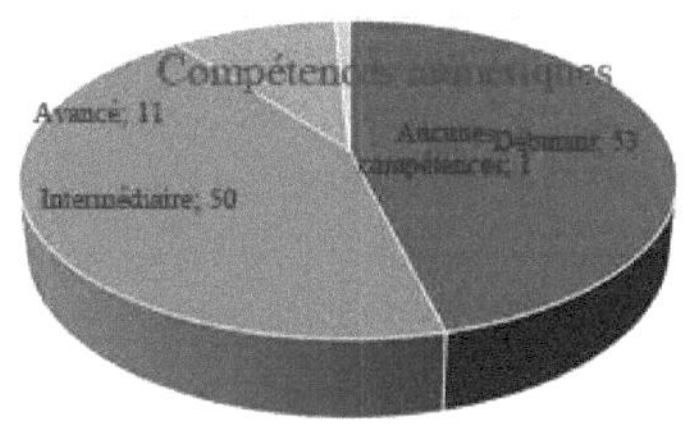

Sources: Data collected by the authors

Overall, this analysis highlights the heterogeneity of digital skills among university students. What's more, 45% of respondents say they have not received any digital training, and 18.10% say they are not familiar with online communication tools such as email, educational discussion forums and videoconferencing. This result illustrates the initial findings and confirms that measures need to be taken to train, support and guide students in the development of digital skills.

Figure 3: Use of digital tools

Use of digital tools

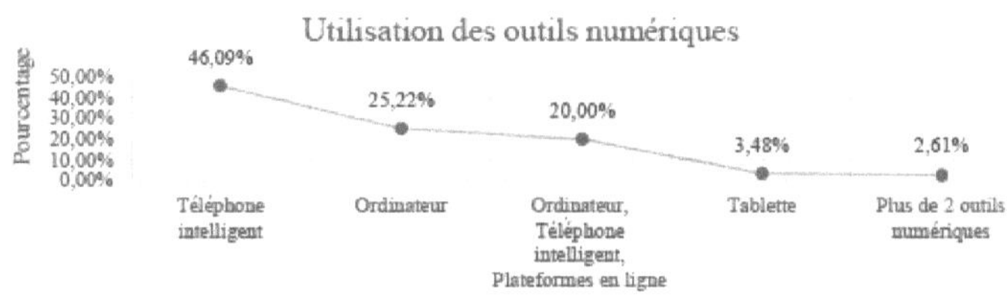

Sources: Data collected by the authors

An analysis of the percentage use of digital tools shows that smartphones are widely used, with 46.09% demonstrating their accessibility and importance. Next come computers, which are used by 25.22% of respondents, maintaining their importance for professional and personal activities that require larger screens and greater processing power. In addition, a significant 20.00% use both a computer and a smartphone, as well as online platforms, suggesting a flexible use of digital tools to meet different needs. Tablets, although less popular, are still used by 3.48% of people, a small proportion of 2.61% use more than two digital tools.

In terms of the reasons why students use digital tools, the data collected revealed that the majority of students (72.12%) use them for various purposes, in particular to search documentation and scientific journals online, to communicate via messaging, email and videoconferencing platforms, to write assignments, etc. 9.62% of students use these tools solely to access online documentation and scientific journals, and 7.69% use them to write assignments using word processing and page layout software. However, only 2.88% say they use digital tools mainly for online learning and participation in webinars. This could indicate a weakness in participation in or organisation of online courses.

The results of the survey indicate that computers are the technology most commonly used by students to access digital tools. Around 45 of the students surveyed said that they mainly use a computer to access technology, while others use smartphones (53 in terms of the number of students), tablets and other digital tools. A significant number of students (49) said that they had not received any outside help in using these digital tools, suggesting a lack of available support. Despite this, the majority of students surveyed reported using technology on a daily basis (75), although many rated their skills as beginner level.

And as far as academic results are concerned, around 60 respondents felt they had good results, suggesting a potential correlation between better access to digital tools and improved academic performance. Students with access to several digital tools and a computer tend to have better academic results (Excellent and Good). We also note a smaller number of respondents with excellent academic results who only have access to the Internet or a telephone, although a number of other factors may influence academic success.

A significant number of students do not have access to computers and a reliable Internet connection, which can have an impact on their learning capacity and limit their access to online resources and courses. While some students (between 23% and 45%) have access to digital tools and skills[1] , there are significant inequalities that affect their academic success. The number of students who consider that they have only a basic level of digital skills is significant (46%). This limited competence could hinder their effective use of technological tools as part of their training, despite a basic understanding. According to the statistics, this does not prevent them from using digital tools, particularly for research, communication and writing. However, a small percentage use these tools for online learning, indicating limited participation in online courses or a lack of opportunities in this area. This may be due to a lack of infrastructure or pedagogical support for online courses in the target institutions.

As far as access to the Internet is concerned, it is more common on the premises of some HEIs than at home, which may force students to stay on campus to access online resources, thus limiting their learning flexibility. Even so, it should be noted that 49% of students say they receive no support in accessing and using digital tools. This may

[1] [illegible]

indicate a degree of self-sufficiency, but it may also point to a lack of institutional support. The data also suggest a correlation between access to various digital tools and good academic results. Students who have regular access to digital tools, particularly computers', seem to achieve better academic results. This tends to imply that digital disparities have an impact on academic performance. Indeed, the lack access to computers, a reliable Internet, and adequate training in digital skills limits the ability of many students to take full advantage of digital learning.

Figure 4: Students' academic results/Average range

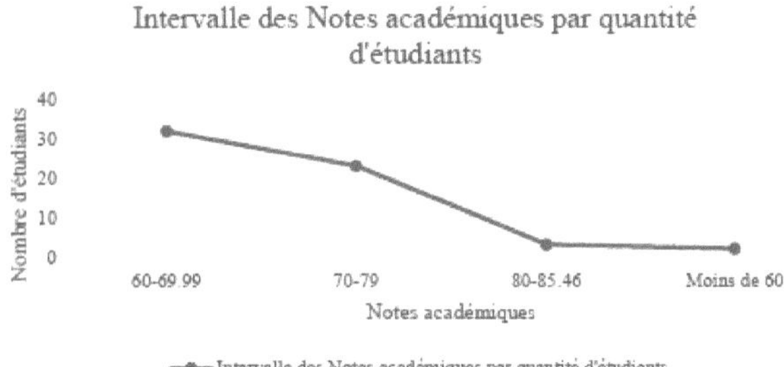

Sources: Data collected by the authors

Analysis of the data shows that 32 students scored between 60 and 69.99, and 2 scored below 60. A proportion of students (23) scored between 70 and 79, and 3 students scored between 80 and 85.46. The median score was 68.14, illustrating the central value of the results, while the standard deviation[2] was 7.49, suggesting a certain dispersion of scores around the mean.

Of the 23 students with academic averages of between 70 and 79, only 5 have full access to digital tools, in this case access to tools, the Internet and a digital infrastructure. They use the tools every day and have levels ranging from intermediate to advanced. 11 of these 23 students have average access and the others have poor access.

Of the 5 students who have between 80 and over, 3 have average access, an intermediate level in terms of digital skills and they use digital tools every day on average.

Of the 33 students who have between 60 and 69.99, 24 have poor access to the Internet, 19 of the 24 consider themselves to be beginners and 17 use digital tools (the few to which they have access) every day. And the remaining 2 who have less than 60 have average access to digital tools, an intermediate level in terms of digital skills and they use the tools every day.

The results indicate that access to digital tools and the level competence in using these tools are important factors in students' academic success. However, they are not the

---

[2]Standard deviation formula: $\sigma = -\Gamma(\Sigma [x - \mu]^2/N)$. Note that the standard deviation was calculated with the help of a µ;v;"; "u"

only determinants, as some students with sufficient access and skills obtain average or poor results, which suggests that other variables need to be taken into account to fully understand the variability in academic performance. Indeed, while access to digital tools and associated skills are important, they need to be considered in conjunction with variables such as level and type of intelligence, cultural background, study environment, academic base, and student engagement. This openness in no way calls into question the impact of the digital divide insofar as the academic base alone, for example, will not be enough to compensate for the lack of skills or access to digital technology.

IV. Challenges of the Digital Transition: Educational governance

Higher education institutions (HEIs) in Jacmel are facing a number of major challenges that could hamper the effective integration of digital technology into teaching and learning practices. These include a lack of material resources, including limited access to computer equipment and essential software, as well a shortage of digital skills and qualified staff. These difficulties compounded by financial constraints that affect the overall process of digital integration. In addition, the lack of a legal framework and institutional policies to govern the use of digital technology in general and in education in particular is holding back the digital transformation.

Digital governance makes it possible to take charge of and strengthen teaching practices, by establishing a regulatory framework for the use of educational technologies. In some countries, new digital laws are encouraging schools to reorganise, making digital governance a key factor in the transformation of teaching practices. This was the case in France, for example, with the Campus numérique 2000-2002 project, which aimed to integrate ICTs into traditional training courses, and the Plan RE/SO 2007[3] launched in 2002, which aimed to digitise face-to-face courses freely.

And also in Italy, with the Codicedell'Amministrazione Digitale[4] code in force from 1 January 2006. This code aims to modernise public administration, including public universities, through the use of technology in administrative procedures. We should also note the Campus One project, which is intended to be the materialisation of a strong commitment by the State to the transformation of universities through ICTs, which are supposed to be in line with the economic and social transformations of the knowledge and information society (presidenza del Consiglio dei Ministri[5] , 28 March 2001 (Thibault and Velez). This raises the question of the need to put in place appropriate institutional policies to design and implement these educational policies effectively.

Digital educational governance supports teaching practices and, more broadly, the process of digital transformation. It implies a political and institutional will to integrate digital technology strategically and critically. This involves defining the issues and

---

[3] Ref to be added.
[4] Digital Administration Code.
[5] T>-A"; J   л

reorganising institutional policies in relation to digital technology, as well as allocating adequate resources and training the players involved. As Lise Vieira points out, "governance thus appears as a method by which actors reach mutually satisfactory decisions through a set of regulatory procedures, via negotiation and cooperation" (Mocquet 30). This definition allows us to understand that digital governance in education refers to the way in which stakeholders within the academic institution coordinate and manage their resources to promote digital development. Digital governance at university level in Haiti faces many challenges due to the country's socio-cultural and economic realities, as well as the lack of a specific legislative framework for digital issues.

"The Haitian education system certainly defines educational policy actions, but these are not framed by a public policy whose continuity and implementation are supposed to be guaranteed, whatever the government in place, unless it is revised with a view to better application for better results" (Renauld 56). And "[...] the weakness of education policies stems from a problem of public governance in general. Existing policies do not tackle the real problems and do not act on irregularities in such a way as to reduce the discrepancies observed in the standards of school operation" (Renauld 56).

In Haiti, the education system is currently undergoing an unprecedented crisis, which requires a reform of its governance, particularly within the Ministry of National Education and Vocational Training. In addition, legislation on the use of information and communication technologies is poor and scattered.

Moreover, there is currently no Digital Code in the country. Knowledge of the rules governing interaction and digital technologies remains difficult. Note, however, the existence of the Order of 9 July 2014 creating the Interministerial Committee on Information Technologies. According to this decree, this committee is responsible for coordinating and harmonising public policies in the field of information technologies, the related y basic infrastructures and the necessary administrative functionalities as well as supervising the implementation of the guiding principles approved by the government. The Ministry of l'Éducation Nationale et de la Formation Professionnelle (MENFP), a member of the aforementioned committee, should a priori promote the use of ICTs in education and identify the needs of state and public universities with regard to such use.

Mention should also be made of the decree of 29 January 2016, through which the Haitian State recognised the right of any citizen to address the public administration electronically. This text lays the legal foundations for the digitisation of public services and the State through ICTs, but requires other laws to complete it. It is important to note, however, that drafting and enacting these laws is not enough if they cannot be implemented. And for good reason, digital law in Haiti faces many challenges, not least a lack of regulation and training for professionals and players in the digital sector. The governance of digital education in Haiti, like the legal texts, faces many challenges, such as the virtual absence of government digital education policies, the inadequacy of communications infrastructures, the lack of teacher training, and so on.

V. **Conclusion**

Digital tools offer new, more up-to-date and modern ways of looking at learning and teaching. This new perception resulting from the integration of digital tools enables universities improve their teaching methods. Where appropriate, they can adapt to the needs of students and to crisis situations, such as the insecurity in Port-au-Prince, where some professors live.

In addition, these tools enrich teaching by increasing the level of retention thanks to digital media, and by making lessons more dynamic thanks to interactive tools. These tools modemise teaching while enhancing learning, and make lessons more lively and interesting thanks to interactive elements that facilitate comprehension: interactive videos, league table quizzes, interactive digital boards.

Digital transformation is dynamic, because it is geared towards a sustainable transition in the integration of digital technology into higher education. It is important to consider current practices and how they can adapt and take advantage of digital technology as much as possible. This also means aiming for continuous improvement combining pedagogy and digital technology.

Combining pedagogy with digital technology means adopting a teaching approach that focuses on the benefits of using digital tools, putting learners at the centre and adapting the tools to their pedagogical needs and learning . To do this, the players involved, and teachers in particular, need to have the skills they need to use the tools effectively; in other words, to integrate them appropriately into their teaching, learning or management practices.

The results of the study show that students have limited access to digital tools and the weather, and that the differences between the level integration of digital tools in the various HEIs designed contribute to reinforcing the digital divide for some and creating it for others. The use of smartphones is very common, according to respondents. And while they reduce the barrier to access by virtue of their many features, including better accessibility than computers, for example, and better access to the Internet through a pay-as-you-go mobile phone network plan, there is a real risk of distraction because of all the games applications and the appeal of social networking.

Many students do use smartphones, but these devices are only used for academic purposes on an ad hoc basis, as their primary function is not education. The vast majority of students have basic digital skills. However, students will need more than these basic skills if they are to manage databases, work on collaborative projects using interactive tools, and create graphical tables, to name but a few. The data also reveals a relationship between access to digital tools and good academic results.

Technological tools open up new perspectives in terms of educational practices. However, they can also create disparities between those who have access and those who are excluded. To ensure equitable and inclusive use, it is essential to take steps to reduce this divide, which is not without consequences. This could include setting up a dedicated IES platform to centralise the resources, tools and information needed to teach and manage digital activities; introducing interactive methods in course delivery to stimulate participation; installing a free and reliable Wi-Fi network throughout the university to allow students easy access to online resources and to conduct their research; and providing access to a digital library at the University.

This includes increasing access to a wide range of digital resources, such as e-books, research articles and specialist databases, and organising regular training workshops to enhance the digital skills of students and staff, with an emphasis on the effective use of digital tools, particularly the technological tools used in teaching.

At the same time, it would be important to teach digital citizenship to students so that they understand that they have responsibilities in using the tools, that they must adopt secure, ethical and eco-responsible behaviour, and communicate responsibly. This also includes promoting the development of a legal framework for the sustainable development aspects of digital technology and mapping the digital players in education.

It would also be crucial to think about adapting digital tools to subjects according to their own specificities so as to have a digital pedagogy that puts the learner at the centre and not the tool. Encouraging research activities (qualitative and quantitative surveys, etc.) in HEIs on the use of digital technology in education would provide contextually relevant and up-to-date data.

Bibliography

1   . Bates, T. *Teaching in the digital age. The nature of knowledge and implications for teaching: Connectivism.* 2022.

2   . Ben Youssef, Adel and Alain Rallet. "ICT in higher education. *Réseaux* 2009.

3   . Ben Youssef, Adel and Mounir Dahmani. "The Impact of ICT on Student Performance in Higher Education: Direct Effects, Indirect Effects and Organisational Change." *RUSC Universities and Knowledge Society Journal* April 2008.

4   . Blamont, J. *For an education revolution in Haiti.* Università d'État d'Haiti, 2013.

5   . Brotcome, P. and G. Valenduc. "Digital skills and inequalities in the use of intemet: How can these inequalities be reduced?" *Les Cahiers du numérique* 2009: 45.< https://www.caim.info/revue-les- cahiers-du-numerique-2009-1->.

6   . Jean Evulu, Oleko. *Les théories de l'apprentissage.* Lodja, Congo- Kinshasa: Università des Sciences et des Technologies de Lodja, 2024. hal- 04587345.

7   . Jean Loisier. *Do the new learning really encourage the performance and success of distance education students?* Réseau d'enseignement francophone à distance du Canada (REFAD). 2011.

8   . Jean-Jacques, N. and B. Oxiné. "Education par le numérique en Haiti: enjeux, défis et perspectives." 2015.

9   . Kazimierz, W. &. - T. "Current status and solutions for digital transformation in Vietnam's education sector." *Research Gate* 2024.

10 Kem, A. - L. "From medium to intermediate city: the dynamics of Jacmel and its positioning in Haiti." 1 January 2019: 267-288.

11 Kem, Abigail-Laure. "From medium to intermediate city: the dynamics of Jacmel and its positioning in Haiti.*" Les Cahiers d'Outre-Mer* 1 January 2019: 267-288.

12 Khöi, L. T. "Theory and concepts". *Education: cultures and societies* 1991: 23-52.

13 Martins, Carlos Benedito. "Higher education in the age of globalization.*" Socio* 2019: 205-227.

14 Michaut, C. "Etat des recherches en économie et en sociologie sur la réussite universitarie." *Educational Research* 15 June 2023: 52. <http ://j oumals .openedition .org/ree/11961>.

15 Mocquet, Bertrand. "University governance and the evolution of digital uses: new challenges for French higher education and research. Information and communication sciences." *HAL Open science* (2017).   <https://theses.hal.science/tel-01758565/file/These_Bertrand_MOCQUET.pdf>.

16 Renauld, Govain. "From the crisis in education to the crisis in education in Haiti." *Caribbean Studies*   December   2023. < http://joumals.openedition.org/etudescaribeennes/28508>.

17 René, Llored. "Education, culture and domination in the sociology of Pierre Bourdieu." 29 June 2022.

18 Thibault, Françoise and Luis Rivera Velez. "PUBLIC POLICIES FOR THE DIGITAL   IN   EDUCATION HIGHER EDUCATION: A comparative study of Spain, France, Italy and the United Kingdom". 2015.

19 Van Dijk, Jan, "The Deepening Divide: Inequality in the Information Society". January 2005.

ICT in higher education: an overview of the practices and perceptions of higher education teachers in Haiti

Mr Anderson TURIN
Research assistant at CRS-IUS in Haiti

Dr Léonard COLIN
Associate researcher, CRS-IUS d'Haiti

Introduction

Since the widespread development Intemet in the 1990s, information and communication technologies (ICTs) have taken off in leaps and bounds, revolutionising today's societies by infiltrating all areas of human life y including education (Mastafi).

With regard to teaching, a number of studies recognise the ability of ICT to innovate teaching practices, empower students and contribute to quality education (El Kartouti and Juidette, 2023; UNESCO, 2018; Lefebvre and Fournier, 2014; Marton, 1999). Moreover, ICTs are proving to be essential tools for guaranteeing educational continuity in emergency situations. The COVID 19 pandemic is a pertinent illustration of this, as it has prompted governments and educational establishments around the world to adopt open distance learning systems mediated by ICT (Bice et al - Donni a - Karsenti et al), through the Ministry of National Education and Vocational Training (MENFP), is encouraging the adoption of ICTs in education, notably in the Pian opérationnel 2010-2015 (MENFP, 2011), in the Politique Nationale de Formation d'Enseignant(e)s et des Personnels d'Encadrement (MENFP, 2018) and in the Pian décennal d'éducation et de formation (PDEF) 2020-2030 (MENFP, 2020).

However, the effective implementation of these positions comes up against a number of problems, in particular the fact that some teachers find it difficult to use technological tools in the teaching context, or even do not use them at all in everyday life, due to a lack of familiarity (France). There is also the fact that teachers' access to these technologies is limited (France, 2011).

Hence our desire to focus our study on the problem of teachers' perceptions of the integration of ICT into university teaching. We therefore ourselves: how do university teachers perceive the integration of technologies into university teaching?

Through this question, we seek to understand teachers' perceptions of the integration of ICT into higher education, with a particular focus on university education. To achieve this objective, we explore the following aspects:

* The technological practices of university teachers ;
* Teachers' perceived contributions and obstacles to the use of ICT in university teaching ;
* Actions to be taken to strengthen and optimise the use of ICT in education.

To reach the end of our approach, we begin with theoretical and contextual explanations of ICTs, then go on to explain the survey protocol chosen for our survey, and continue with the presentation and analysis of the survey results, before finally discussing the results.

I. Technology integration in education

In the field of technologies applied to education, one might think that the integration of technologies simply means their use by teachers. However, it is clear that it involves more than just use, but use driven by learning objectives (Mastafi, 2016). In other words, integration means adopting a technological tool or tools in order to achieve a learning objective. Therefore, in order to truly talk about the integration of ICT in education, it is essential to involve ICT in a meaningful way in the different learning activities of students (Mastafi, 2016).

Some authors (Lauzon, Michaud and Forgette-Giroux, 1991; Raby, 2004; Mastafi, 2016) distinguish between two main types of integration: physical integration, which consists of making technological equipment available in schools or educational structures, and pedagogical integration, which corresponds to the use of technological tools in teaching and learning. Full integration of technologies would therefore involve both physical and pedagogical integration.

The scientific literature describes several integration processes. We therefore distinguish between Raby's (2004) four-stage model, Puentedura's (2009) SAMR model (substitution, augmentation, modification, redefinition) and Karsenti's (2013) teacher-centred ASPID model (adoption, substitution, progress, innovation, deterioration).

Raby's model proposes a dynamic approach to the adoption of ICT by teachers. This model places strong emphasis on the teacher's intention as being central to the use of ICT. It takes account of the teacher as a whole (the person, the professional, the teacher). This integration seems to place the emphasis on the teacher's perception, which guides his or her choice as to whether or not to adopt the technology. We might conclude that for Raby, the pedagogical adoption a technology by a teacher must first be based on a positive personal and professional experience of digital technology, which could have an influence on the teacher's perception, and therefore on his or her practices.

According to Levy (2017), the SAMR model (Substitution, Augmentation, Modification, Redefinition) puts the student at the centre of learning by using digital tools to serve him or her. Puentedura's model focuses on teaching practices in classroom. It outlines the step-by-step process by which teachers integrate technological tools into their teaching activities. Integration is therefore a process in which each stage corresponds to a greater degree of use of technology in classroom activities.

The ASPID model (Adoption, Substitution, Progress, Innovation, Deterioration), developed by Karsenti (2013), is a model designed to account for the various stages through which the teacher progresses in the quest to integrate ICT into the teaching-learning process.

This model, which in our view is very similar to the one presented by Puentedura, differs in that it takes account of the deterioration phase. The adoption of technology may not be effective for everyone, and there are several reasons for this, perception being one of them, as we shall see below. A bad experience with technology can discourage teachers using it. This aspect needs to be taken into account better plan integration into classrooms.

II. Exploring the pedagogical integration of technology by higher education teachers

To carry out this study, we opted for a mixed approach with a sequential explanatory design, which refers to research in two phases: firstly, a quantitative approach and secondly, a qualitative approach (Bourgeault et al., 2010, p. 24).

For the purposes of this study, our target population was university teachers in the commune of Jacmel, regardless of their status, place of residence or nationality. The nature of the population was determined by the fact that they teach in the university establishments that exist in Jacmel. In the first phase, we collected quantitative data from 38 teachers (10 women and 28 men) who were selected by simple random sampling in order to minimise the risk of bias resulting from the selection of participants that could influence the results (Anadón, 2019). In the second phase, we collected qualitative data from 11 teachers chosen from among those surveyed in the first phase on the basis of their habit of using ICT in their teaching practices. This was non-probabilistic purposive sampling (Ajar et al. 2009).

For this research, we designed two questionnaires: one consisting mainly of closed-ended questions with a view to collecting essentially quantitative data, and the other consisting open-ended questions for collecting verbatim reports. The closed-ended questionnaire was divided into three sections, each serving a specific purpose. The first section, entitled 'General information', contained six items designed to provide a profile of the respondents to the questionnaires (gender, age, level of education, length of service, level of university education, educational establishment).

The second section, entitled "ICT skills", aimed to categorise teachers according to their ability to use ICT on a personal, professional and pedagogical level. The third section of the questionnaire, entitled "Pedagogical use of ICT", aimed to assess the degree use of ICT in university teaching practices through four questions. With regard to the open-ended questionnaire, the general objective was to gather verbatim data in order to understand the advantages and perceived limitations of using ICT and the actions envisaged to promote the use ICT in teaching.

1- Teacher profile: social, professional and digital skills

First of all, let's take a look at the profile of the participants, the vast majority of whom (63.2%) are aged between 30 and 45; the 46 to 60 age group is also important, with a frequency of 28.9%; two teachers (5.3%) are under 30 and one teacher is over 60, accounting for 2.3%.

Age group frequencies			
Age group	Quantities	of total	Cumulative
Under 30	2	5,3 %	5,3 %
Between 30 and 45 years old	24	63,2 %	68,4 %

| Between 46 and 60 | 11 | 28,9 % | 97,4 % |
| More than 60 arn> | 1 | 2,6 % | 100,0 % |

Source: survey of teachers' perceptions of the integration of ICT in higher education.

Among the participants, 65.8% had a Master's degree, 21.1% a Bachelor's degree and 7.9% a DESS. 5.3% had a DESS.

Frequency of Current level of study			
Current level of study	Quantities	of total	Cumulative
DESS	2	5,3 %	5,3 %
Doctorate	8	21,1 %	26,3 %
Licence	3	7,9 %	34,2 %
Master's degree	25	65,8 %	100,0 %

Source: survey of teachers' perceptions of the integration of ICT in higher education

Analysis of the data collected shows that the participating teachers were used to ICT. As regards the uses made of ICT by the teachers, the participants generally use ICT for pedagogical activities (100%) such as lessons, sharing documents, teaching, etc. They also use it to carry out activities of an academic (97.4%), personal (92.1%) and professional (89.4%) nature. They also use it for academic (97.4%), personal (92.1%) and professional (89.5%) activities. These results confirm that technology is used in both personal and professional aspects of teachers' lives.

Figure 1. Teachers' use of ICT

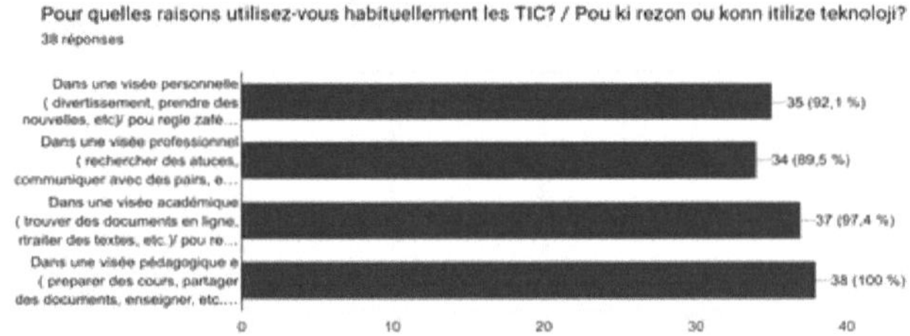

Source: survey of teachers' perceptions of integration of ICT into teaching

superior

2- *Teachers' ICT teaching practices*

At the outset, we were interested in the ICTs that the participating teachers use for their teaching activities. We found that teachers mainly use computers and the Internet. Smartphones, mobile applications, video projectors, websites, desktop software and social networks are also widely used by teachers. However, the least used ICTs are interactive digital whiteboards, online teaching platforms, virtual reality and serious games.

Figure 2. ICT used in teaching practices

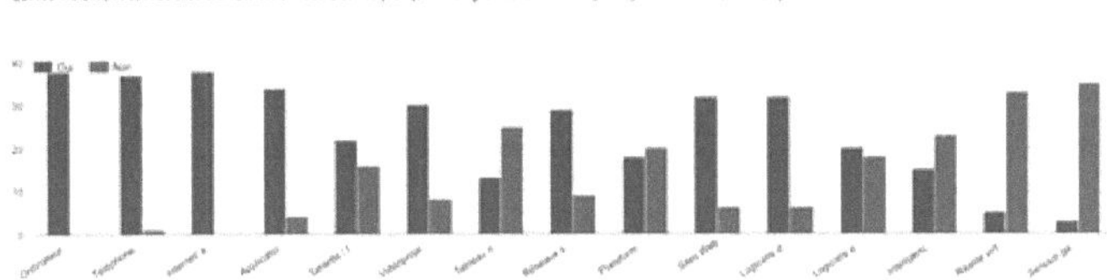

Source: survey of teachers' perceptions of the integration of ICT into higher education.

Participants use ICT to lessons, share documents, carry out research, communicate with students and present knowledge in classroom. Although distance learning and assessment are also practised, their uses remain less frequent than others.

Figure 3. Teaching activities using ICT

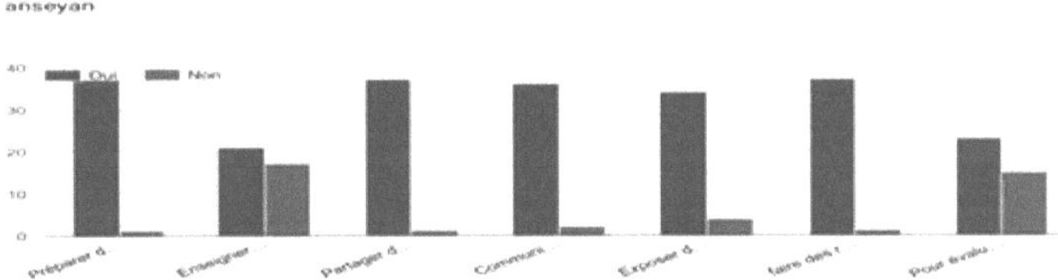

Source: survey of teachers' perceptions of the integration of ICT into higher education.

3- *The benefits of integrating ICT into higher education*

The teachers' responses to the second phase of the survey on the benefits of ICT were as follows: optimisation of productivity, time management, preparation of courses and research, innovative teaching strategies and globalisation teaching.

Indeed, for the respondents, ICTs make it possible optimise teacher productivity and better manage their time, because they simplify activities by carrying out tasks automatically. For teacher Mario, ICTs make it possible to meet "the need to deliver more in record time", and are used to make teachers "more effective".

The teachers' responses also reveal that ICT is useful for lesson preparation. Jacques, for example, mentions that ICT provides "quick and easy access a large amount of information and educational resources... which teachers can use to prepare lessons".

Some teachers point out, based on their experience, that teachers who use ICT benefit from a "document search" offering them a wide range of resources to enrich their lessons.

The teachers' responses reveal the contribution of ICT to the effectiveness and innovation of teaching strategies. "ICT makes it easier to transfer knowledge from one person to another than the traditional system", said Néhémy. With ICT, "transmission is easier and quicker", according to Stéphane. For Judith, ICTs make it possible to "benefit from the latest innovations". With the many educational tools and resources available, teachers are able to implement strategies to improve their teaching. As part of this process of innovation, Stéphane points out that "with ICT, teachers become global, they can stay at home and teach in any country".

The global aspect mentioned above also underlines the fact that integrating technology into the teaching process enables teachers to become part of the modern world, since the use of ICT implies the development of digital skills. According to the participants, ICT enables teachers to establish connections with different people around the world. According to Mardochée, they enable teachers to "move with the world" and, according to Liliane, to "participate in the evolution of the world".

As far as the benefits for learners are concerned, James believes that it "increases engagement and motivation" among learners. According to Stéphane, "The course is more lively", while James observes that "The students are more motivated, they take the course more seriously". These extracts from the respondents' answers sum up the perceived contribution of integrating ICT to optimising interactivity and learner engagement in the learning process.

According to the same results, learners become more productive: they find ways to complete complex tasks in a short time and with minimum effort, which represents a "saving energy". According to Saincy, "ICT helps students with the presentation of assignments given by teachers. They also allow them deepen their knowledge". With ICT, they "can work quickly and efficiently", says Johnny. What's more, they need less time to assimilate new concepts. So learners are much more efficient.

The third benefit of ICTs for learners, according to the respondents, is increased autonomy in learning. Néhémy points out that internet provides students with a wide range of information that they can consult to enhance their knowledge and delve deeper. He adds that ICTs "facilitate self-learning", because they enable participants progress autonomously. This autonomy is also reflected in Jacques' statement that students have "access to relevant information" and can "do a quick search". As a result, learners are not totally dependent on teachers for their learning; they can teach themselves.

The respondents' answers focus on the adaptability and accessibility of learning, which refers broadly to the flexibility that learners benefit from thanks to ICTs. Stéphane states this by saying that "the learner can listen to the corns again at any time". For Liliane, "students can stay at home to follow the course and won't have to pay for transport". Néhémy agrees, pointing out that "students can learn at home, and the cost of learning is reduced". In fact, technology offers wide access to training programmes that can be accessed online, considerably reducing the cost for learners. They no longer need to travel and be physically present to attend the course in classroom.

4- Obstacles and strategies for ¡integrating ICT into higher education

As obstacles to the integration ICT into university teaching, teachers highlighted the poor quality and quantity infrastructure and energy resources. James points out that: e To use technology in university teaching, the teacher needs the internet, a computer, a projector or an interactive digital board. [Depending on] the content to be taught, if these tools are not available, the teacher will not be able to use the technologies". In his view, the use of ICTs in university teaching requires an appropriate set of materials to ensure effective use. In this sense, Judith, Liliane and Mario point out that "rudimentary" and "mediocre" Internet connections and "energy problems" are obstacles to the integration of ICT into teaching.

The results show that teachers' lack of skills is a key obstacle to the integration of ICT into university teaching. "Among the reasons for this is the fact that some teachers are not up to date with modern technologies," says Liliane. This lack of skills is linked to a lack of knowledge of the technologies that exist, a lack of ability to handle the equipment and a lack of knowledge of how to use ICT for learning.

ICT dependency is another category of barrier. According to Jacques *e the* constant use of technology can lead to over-dependence on the part of students, which their ability to think independently. The second reason is that technology can be a source of distraction for students, preventing them from concentrating on learning activities.

The "lack of resources" cited by Stéphane and "the cost of subscriptions, tools and equipment" listed by Liliane is another obstacle. The respondents felt that the limited financial resources available to decision-makers and teachers to purchase equipment prevented the use of technology in education.

As part of this research, the participants were also asked to suggest parameters on which to act in order to bring about a general and real integration of technologies into university teaching.

All the participants confirmed that infrastructure and technological resources need to be made available. Not only do we need, as Liliane points out, "equipment and above all a better quality internet network throughout Haiti". But also, as James points out, universities need to "make available the infrastructure needed to use ICTs, such as the internet, energy, computers, tablets and computer software". There also needs to be "electricity and a good connection", "virtual libraries" and so on, so that teachers can have access to these tools. Given the cost involved, respondents suggested "financing the purchase of teaching equipment".

"Each university must make the tools available to teachers and train them to use them," says James. This strategy was also put forward by several teachers. Likewise, Saincy believes that "training in the proper use of ICTs would be a great help to both teachers and students". For Johnny, we need to "put in place a structure responsible for training users". The training aims both to "raise teachers' awareness of the importance of ICT at university" and to "teach teachers how to use the various equipment".

III. State of play and perceptions of higher education teachers regarding the pedagogical integration of ICT

The main aim of this research was to examine how university teachers perceive the integration of technology into teaching. Although this is a topical issue, its roots go back many years. We sought to describe teachers' teaching practices in a context where digital technology is omnipresent, to understand their perceptions of ICT in terms of its benefits and limitations, and to generate ideas for action to improve the integration of ICT into the Haitian education system.

1. Teachers' technological practices

The results show that teachers use varying degrees integration of technology in their teaching practices, illustrating a diversity approaches to the use of ICT. Teachers use ICT as a means of accessing documents to prepare lessons. But also as a tool for presenting lessons in the . In fact, ICT is used more as a teaching aid. These results are in line with those of other studies, such as Guichon (2012), which was conducted by questionnaire among 180 secondary school language teachers in France, and the study by Roland and Vanmeerhaeghe among 66 higher education teachers in Wallonia-Brussels in Belgium, which concluded that teachers use ICT mainly to enrich lessons with authentic digital documents and to ask students to carry out research.

Similarly, the results show that ICT is used not only to ensure communication between teachers and students outside the classroom, but also to enable students to share resources.

However, not many teachers use ICT to assess or teach at a distance. We are tempted to explain this by the fact that teachers are not trained in distance learning platforms and distance assessment software.

This research also reveals that teachers make greater use of mobile technologies such as computers, smartphones, tablets, mobile applications and others. These technologies are generally very widespread in professional environments because they are mobile and make it possible to reduce time and space constraints (Loup et al.).

2. Perception of ¡ICT use in education

Teachers recognise that ICT enormous benefits, including increased productivity, greater accessibility, increased interactivity, autonomy and student engagement. There is also an improvement the way lessons are prepared.

A number of studies confirm these contributions, including Dahmani and Ragni (2009), who summarised a number of scientific studies and concluded that ICTs enable students to make better use of the time they devote to student work and enable students who are constrained either by their professional activities, geographical location or financial situation to access courses that would not be possible in the traditional way. Coutaz (2013, cited in Riyami) notes that ICTs interactivity between learners and teachers. As well as improving learner commitment and optimising their autonomy, learners are therefore involved in their own learning and feel that they have a stake in it.

These perceived contributions show that teachers have a practical vision of ICT. They do not see it as an artefact that can replace them, but as a tool to serve their profession. However, they also point to limits to the physical and pedagogical integration of ICT in higher education. Teachers cite the lack and poor quality/quantity of technological equipment as an obstacle to the use of ICT. The British Educational Communications and Technology Agency (BECTA), on the basis of a literature review, mentioned, as did the teachers in our study, the lack of equipment in terms of quality and quantity as a challenge to the integration of ICT. BECTA (2004) states that teachers' lack of access to resources can take several forms: lack of equipment, poor organisation of resources, poor quality equipment, inappropriate software, lack of personal access for teachers.

The problem of teachers' lack of competence in exploiting the pedagogical potential of ICT often recurs in the literature as a challenge to integrating ICT into teaching (BECTA, 2004; UNESCO, 2023; Guichon, 2012). Our results also point in this direction. Indeed, the lack of skills was mentioned as an obstacle in the teachers' comments. On this point, lack of competence combines teachers' poor knowledge of ICTs, their limited ability to handle them, and their lack of professional training in the use of ICTs.

To improve the integration of ICT, teachers proposed several strategies. These include the need to make technological infrastructures available. These infrastructures are not limited to schools. It is a national measure, covering the whole of Haiti. On this point, UNESCO recognises that connectivity and availability, among other things, are important to ensure that ICTs integrated into higher education. In fact, it recommends that governments should "broaden access to the Internet so that not only are higher education institutions equipped with a good Internet connection, but it must also be available and affordable on an individual scale" (UNESCO, 2023, p. 117).

Participants stressed the importance of in-service training to ensure that teachers are comfortable with digital tools. To begin with, they called for training to prepare teachers to use ICTs; it would seem that this is initial training that all universities should provide before teachers even start work. Next, they propose the creation of a structure within the university to provide assistance to teachers. Finally, they recommend in-service training sessions to keep teachers and students up to date. These recommendations are in line with those made by UNESCO (2023) to ensure the integration ICT into higher education. It recommends, for example, continuing training for university staff, awareness-raising among teaching staff, hiring specialists to ensure the implementation of ICT in teaching and to support teachers, and requiring ICT training for students to encourage teachers to take further training in order to keep up to date (UNESCO, 2023, p. 117).

Conclusion

In conclusion, this research provides an overview of the integration of ICT into the teaching practices of university teachers. The results show that teachers are used to using technological tools and resources. They have access to a wide variety of ICTs, but are more familiar with mobile technologies than with recent technologies such as virtual reality and artificial intelligence. In terms of their teaching practices, they use ICT to prepare lessons, support presentation, and communicate and share resources with learners.

On the other hand, this research highlights the varied perceptions teachers regarding the integration of ICT into higher education.

They say that integrating ICT into higher education improves the quality of teaching by facilitating access to resources, making courses more interactive, and making learners more motivated, engaged and autonomous in their learning. They offer more learning options, in particular by facilitating access to training programmes tailored to learners and teachers. Not mention making it easier to enter the fully connected world. Despite this positive view of ICT, teachers cite persistent challenges, such the lack of training in the pedagogical use of ICT, as well as the shortage or absence of resources, and the low quality of those available. These obstacles, coupled with student dependence and the high cost of ICT, can limit or even bioquer the use of technological tools in their teaching practices. Consequently, if ICT is to be successfully integrated, initiatives need to be put in place to facilitate the implementation of technological resources and equipment throughout the country and in educational establishments. Training in the use of technology in education is also recommended. Finally, a strategic plan for the integration of ICT is essential.

The results of this study can be used as a basis for developing strategies to strengthen the integration of ICT into the Haitian education system, taking into account the needs and expectations of teachers.

Bibliography

1   . Bice, Matthew R., et al. Teaching at a distance: faculty initiatives during the pandemic. International Journal of Technologies in University Education, vol. 17, no. 2, 2020, pp. 97-103. DOI.org (Crossref), https://doi.org/10.18162/ritpu-2020-v17n2-10.

2   . Bourgault, Patricia, et al. Le devis mixte en sciences infirmières ou quand une question de recherche appelle des stratégies qualitatives et quantitatives". Recherche en soins infirmiers, vol. 103, no 4, 2010, p. 20-28. Cairn.info, https://doi.org/10.3917/rsi.103.0020 .

3   . British Educational Communications and Technology Agency. A review of the research literature on barriers to the uptake of ICT by teachers. 2004, p. 29,

https://dera.ioe .ac .uk/id/eprint/1603/1/becta_2004_barrierstouptake_litrev. pdf.

4   . Dahmani, Mounir, and Ludovic Ragni. "The impact of information and communication technologies on student performance". Réseaux, vol. 155,   no.   3, 2009, p. 81-110. Cairn.info,

https://doi.org/10.3917/res.155.0081.

5   . Dounla, Michel Fayole, "WhatsApp et continuità pédagogique à l'ère de la COVID 19: l'exemple de l'Université internationale Jean-Paul II et de l'Institut universitarie royal de Baboutcha-Nintcheu (Cameroun)". Revue internationale des technologies en pédagogie universitarie, voi. 19, no 2, 2022, p. 61-73. DOI.org (Crossref), https://doi.org/10.18162/ritpu-2022- v19n2-05 .

6   . El Kartouti, Salah Eddine, and Sarah Juidette. "The impact of the use of ICT in education on improving the learning of schoolchildren, and the consequences for the environment." SHS Web of Conferences, edited by S. Bourekkadi et al, voi. 175, 2023, p. 01015. DOI.org (Crossref), https://doi.org/10.1051/shsconf/202317501015 .

7   . France, Pierre A. N. Etzer. ICT and the training of primary school teachers in Haiti: barriers and facilitating factors. 2011. Université de Montréal.

8   . Guichon, Nicolas. Towards the integration of ICT in language teaching.

Didier   FLE, 2012. DOI.org (Crossref), https://doi.org/10.14375/NP.9782278072125.

9   . Karsenti, Thierry. "Le modéle ASPID : modéliser le processus d'adoption et d'intégration pédagogique des technologies en contexte éducatif". Formation et profession, vol. 21, no 1, 2013, p. 74-75.

10 .-. " Le numérique et l'enseignement au temps de la COVID-19 : entre défis et perspectives - Partie 1". International Journal of Technologies in University Education, vol. 17, no. 2, 2020, pp. 1-4. DOI.org (Crossref), https://doi.org/10.18162/ritpu-2020-v17n2-01 .

H.Lefebvre, Sonia, and Hélène Fournier. "Utilisations personnelles, professionnelles et pédagogiques des TIC par de futurs enseignants et des enseignants". Revue internationale des technologies en pédagogie universitaire, vol. 11, no. 2, 2014, p. 38. DOI.org (Crossref), https://doi.org/10.7202/1035634ar .

12 Levy, Alain. "SAMR, un modéle à suivre pour développer le numérique éducatif". Technologie, no 206, January 2017, p. 8-13.

13 Loup,   Pierre, and   al.   "Role des   technologies nómades.   The relations

interpersonal skills in sales teams". Organisational Technology Management, vol. 7, no 2, 2017, pp. 137-51.

14 Marton, Philippe. "Information and communication technologies and their future in education". Education et francophonie, vol.   27, no 2,   1999, p.   1.
DOI.org (Crossref),
https://doi.org/10.7202/1080489ar.

15 Mastafi, Mohammed. ICT(E) definitions and acception. L'Harmattan, 2016.   hal-amu.archives-ouvertes.fr,   https://hal-amu.archives-ouvertes.fr/hal-02048883.

16 Ministry of Planning and External Cooperation. Haiti's Strategic Development : Emerging Country 2030. 2012.

17 Ministry of National Education and Vocational Training. Ministerial order creating the MENFP Educational Technology Unit. 2016.

18 .-. The national action strategy for education for all. 2007.

19 .-. Operational Plan 2010-2015. National Library, 2011.

20 .-. National policy for non-formal education in Haiti. 2019.

21 .-. National training policy for teachers and supervisory staff. 2018.

22 United Nations Educational, Scientific and Cultural Organization. UNESCO ICT Competency Framework for Teachers. 3rd edn, UNESCO, 2018.

23 Riyami, Bouchaib. Analysis of the effects of ICT on higher education in Morocco in a training context in collaboration with a French university. 2018. University of Southern Brittany, These. HAL.

24 Roland, Nicolas, and Sophie Vanmeerhaeghe. "Teacher educators facing their students' personal learning environments: representations and accompaniment". Revue internationale de pédagogie de l'enseignement supérieur, voi. 32, no 1, 2016, p. 1-20.

25 .UNESCO. Recommendations for the integration of ICT in education policies. UNESCO, 2023,
https://unesdoc.unesco.Org/ark:/48223/pf0000386039/PDF/386039fre.pdf. multi.

94

Mr Bertrand DESTINE
Dr Philippe SIMON

Quality Banking Services in Haiti: The Impact of Digitalisation on SME Performance in Jacmel

Quality of Banking Services in Haiti: Effect of Digitalization on the Performance of SMEs in Jacmel

Summary

In principle, business performance is determined by a multitude of factors. One of these is the quality of services offered by commercial banks. In this study, we seek determine the effect of digital banking on the performance of SMEs in Jacmel, in a context marked by the scarcity of credit and dysfunctions linked to payments. To this end, we conducted a survey of 118 SMEs in the city. Based on the data collected, we estimated two multiple regression models describing the relationship between the variables studied. Our results show that digital banking has a positive and significant effect on turnover, while the effect on the triptych quality-cost-delivery time for goods or services of SMEs is positive, but not significant. Sales and the quality-cost-delivery time triptych for SME products are the main indicators for measuring this performance.

Key words: Quality, Banking, Performance, SME, Digitalisation.

Dr Christophe PROVIDENCE
Public choice and adoption of mobile money for financial inclusion in Haiti
Public choices and adoption of mobile money for financial inclusion in Haiti
Summary
The adoption of mobile money (MM) has become a key lever for financial inclusion in developing countries. This paper examines the determinants of mobile money adoption in Haiti and its impact on unbanked populations. The results suggest that mobile money can help reduce financial inequality, but that challenges remain, particularly in terms of infrastructure and digital education. An analysis of the adoption of mobile money in Haiti using the theory of incompatible public choices, proposed by Christophe Providence, highlights the tensions between the priorities of the various players and the needs of the population. By overcoming these differences through better coordination, appropriate regulations and targeted investment, it is possible to maximise the potential of mobile money to promote financial inclusion in the country.
Keywords: Financial inclusion, Mobile money, Incompatible public choices, Sustainable development, Haiti

Mr Jerry Rood LUBIN
Dr Christophe PROVIDENCE
An Imbricative Approach to Evaluating the Effectiveness of Health Information Systems in Carrefour, Haiti
An Nesting Approach to Assess the Effectiveness of Health Information Systems in Carrefour, Haiti

Summary

This study uses Christophe Providence's theory of interweaving to analyse the effectiveness of Health Information Systems (HIS) in the municipality of Carrefour, Haiti. Through an exploration of the interactions between the technical, social and organisational dimensions, it identifies the obstacles to the management of electronic medical records (EMR) and proposes integrated solutions. The legal framework for the protection of medical data was examined to identify gaps in existing regulations, while back-up and continuity strategies in the event of incidents were highlighted as crucial to the sustainability of services. The results reveal significant data fragmentation and challenges relating to interoperability, infrastructure and training. Using a methodology inspired by nesting theory, this research offers strategic recommendations for aligning local practices with international standards.

Keywords: health information system, electronic medical records, electronic data management, medical data protection, nesting theory

Ms Rachelle CHARLES
Dr Jean Rony GUSTAVE

ICT in higher education: Impact of the digital divide on academic performance

ICT in higher education: Impact of the digital divide on academic performance

Summary

Since their integration into higher education, information and communication technologies (ICTs) have been transforming teaching practices, administrative processes and the university experience more generally. However, the challenges associated with the digital divide tend to undermine these impacts, highlighting inequalities in access to and use of digital tools. Using a data collection approach combining exploratory and quantitative analysis, this study looks at the use of digital tools in teaching and management and their actual influence on students' academic results. The findings show that the impact of digital technology on learning is multidimensional. In addition to its use, other factors need to be considered, including socio-demographic characteristics, living conditions, professional activities, previous schooling, learning methods and study contexts.

Keywords: Digital inclusion, Higher education, Digital divide, Digital governance, Digital policy, Digital skills

Mr Anderson TURIN
Dr Léonard COLIN
ICT in higher education: an overview of the practices and perceptions of higher education teachers in Haiti
ICT in higher education: inventory of practices and perceptions of higher education teachers in Haiti

Summary

This article focuses on the integration Information and Communication Technologies (ICT) into university teaching. It presents the results of a mixed-methods study carried out in Haiti, aimed at understanding teachers' perceptions. The study explores their pedagogical practices, the perceived benefits and obstacles of ICT integration, and recommendations for promoting effective adoption of these technologies. We conducted a two-phase field survey using questionnaires: a quantitative phase with 38 university teachers and a qualitative phase with 11 university teachers.

Keywords: ICT, perception, integration, pedagogical integration, pedagogical practices, higher education, university

Printed by Books on Demand GmbH, Norderstedt / Germany